Be My Disciples

Peter M. Esposito
President

Jo Rotunno, MA
Publisher

Susan Smith
Director of Project Development

Program Advisors
Michael P. Horan, PhD
Elizabeth Nagel, SSD

GRADE TWO
PARISH EDITION

The Subcommittee on the Catechism, United States Conference of Catholic Bishops, has found this catechetical series, copyright 2013, to be in conformity with the *Catechism of the Catholic Church*.

NIHIL OBSTAT
Rev. Msgr. Robert Coerver
Censor Librorum

IMPRIMATUR
† Most Reverend Kevin J. Farrell, DD
Bishop of Dallas
August 22, 2011

The *Nihil Obstat and Imprimatur* are official declarations that the material reviewed is free of doctrinal or moral error. No implication is contained therein that those granting the *Nihil Obstat and Imprimatur* agree with the contents, opinions, or statements expressed.

Acknowledgments

Excerpts are taken and adapted from the *New American Bible* with Revised New Testament and Revised Psalms © 1991, 1986, 1970, Confraternity of Christian Doctrine, Washington, D.C., and are used by permission. All Rights Reserved. No part of the *New American Bible* may be reproduced in any form without permission in writing from the copyright owner.

Excerpts are taken and adapted from the English translation of the *Roman Missal*, © 2010, International Commission on English in the Liturgy, Inc. (ICEL). All rights reserved.

Excerpts and adaptations of prayers were taken from the book of *Catholic Household Blessings & Prayers*, © 2007, United States Conference of Catholic Bishops, Washington, D.C. All rights reserved. No part of the book of *Catholic Household Blessings & Prayers* may be reproduced or transmitted in any form or by any means, electronic or mechanical, including photocopying, recording, or by any information storage and retrieval system, without permission in writing from the copyright holder.

Toll Free   877-275-4725
Fax   800-688-8356

Visit us at www.RCLBenziger.com
and www.BeMyDisciples.com

20702 ISBN 978-0-7829-1571-6 (Student Edition)
20712 ISBN 978-0-7829-1577-8 (Catechist Edition)

4th Printing.
March 2015.

Contents

Welcome to
Be My Disciples

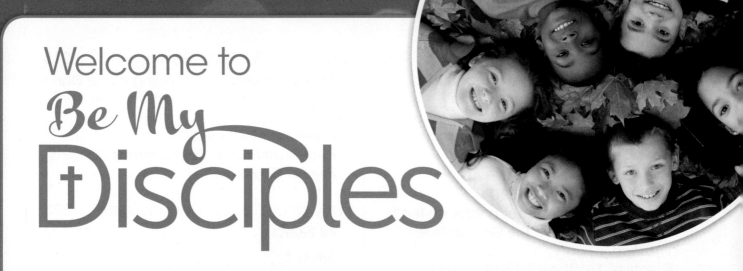

A Few Facts About Me

My name is _____.

My favorite story is _____.

My favorite holiday is _____.

I am good at _____.

New Things to Learn

This year we will learn many new things about God. We will learn more about Jesus and how to celebrate with our Church family.

Play this game with a partner to begin to learn new things. As you come to each text box, write the answer to the question.

Unit 1: We Believe, Part One

God is the Father and Creator. He made everyone and everything out of love, without any help.
Write the word that means only God has the power to do

everything good. _____

Clue: Look on page 37.

Unit 2: We Believe, Part Two

Jesus is God's own Son. He is the Savior of the world.

Write the word that means "God saves." _____

Clue: Look on page 57.

Unit 3: We Worship, Part One

The Sacraments are seven signs of God's love for us. We share in God's love when we celebrate the Sacraments. Write the word that means to honor and love God above

all else. _____

Clue: Look on page 85.

Unit 4: We Worship, Part Two

At Mass, we listen to God's Word and give thanks to him.

What is a word we sing before the Gospel at Mass? _____

Clue: Look on page 129.

Unit 5: We Live, Part One

We live as children of God when we live the Great Commandment. The Great Commandment sums up all of God's laws.

What is a sign of how Jesus lived the Great Commandment?

_____

Clue: Look on page 167.

Unit 6: We Live, Part Two

The Our Father is the prayer of the whole Church.

Find the word that means "Yes, it is true. We believe!" _____

Clue: Look on page 219.

Enough for Everyone

Leader   We gather to praise your Word, O Lord.

All   **Thank you for the gift of your Word.**

Leader   A reading from the holy Gospel according to Luke.

All   **Glory to you, O Lord.**

Leader   One day a large crowd of people was listening to Jesus. That evening Jesus said, "Where can we get enough food for all these people?" His disciple Andrew said, "There is a boy here with five loaves of bread and two fish, but what good will that do?" Jesus said, "Tell the people to sit down." Then he took the bread and fish and gave thanks to God. He passed out the food to all the people who were there. When everyone was full, he asked the disciples to pick up the food that was left over. They collected twelve baskets of bread.

BASED ON JOHN 6:1-13

The Gospel of the Lord.

All   **Praise to you, Lord Jesus Christ.**

Leader   Come forward in a line and bow before the Bible.

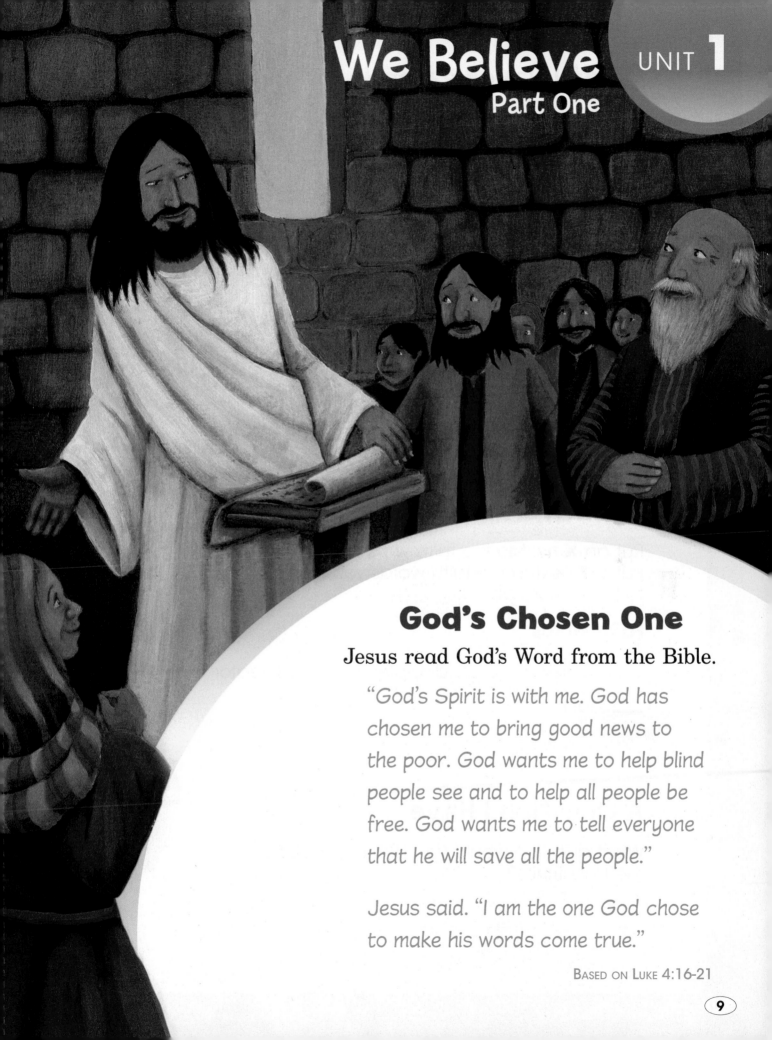

We Believe
Part One

God's Chosen One

Jesus read God's Word from the Bible.

"God's Spirit is with me. God has chosen me to bring good news to the poor. God wants me to help blind people see and to help all people be free. God wants me to tell everyone that he will save all the people."

Jesus said. "I am the one God chose to make his words come true."

BASED ON LUKE 4:16-21

What I Have Learned

What is something you already know about these faith concepts?

the Bible

_____

_____

the Holy Trinity

_____

_____

Faith Words to Know

Put an **X** next to the faith words you know.
Put a **?** next to the faith words you need
to learn more about.

Faith Words

____ believe   ____ disciples   ____ Creator

____ faith   ____ soul

A Question I Have

What question would you like to ask about
the Holy Trinity?

_____

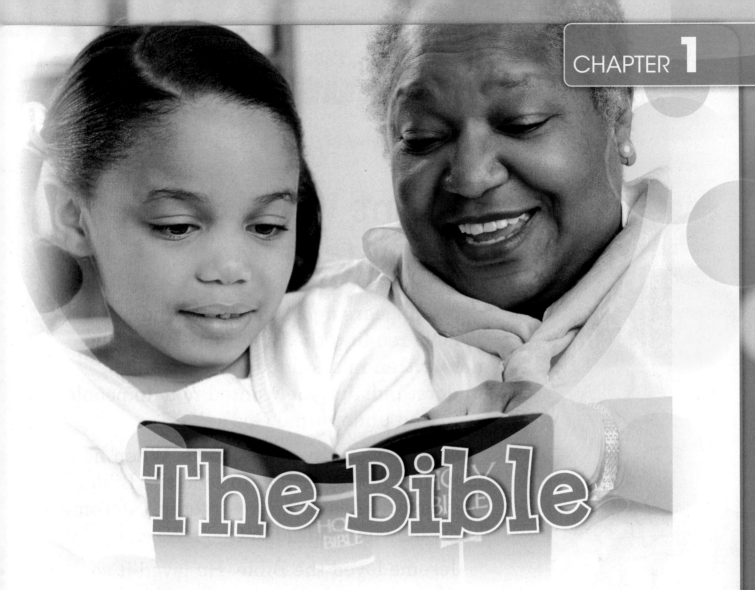

CHAPTER 1

The Bible

? What is your favorite story? What is your favorite Bible story?

When we listen to stories from the Bible, we listen to God speaking to us. Listen to what God is telling us in these words from the Bible.

Long ago, God spoke to people who lived before us. He spoke in many different ways. Now God talks to us through his own Son, Jesus. BASED ON HEBREWS 1:1-2

? What do you think God is saying to you in these words from the Bible?

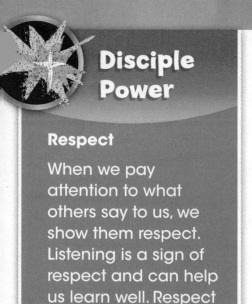

Respect

When we pay attention to what others say to us, we show them respect. Listening is a sign of respect and can help us learn well. Respect for others is a way we show God's love.

The Church Follows
Jesus

A Saint Who Loved the Bible

Many years ago, some people had trouble reading the Bible. The Bible was not written in a language they could understand. Jerome wanted to help people read and understand God's Word.

Jerome went to good schools. When he grew up, Jerome began to read the Bible. He respected what he was reading. Jerome knew he was reading to God's Word.

Jerome loved the Bible. He loved it so much he wanted other people to read it and learn to love it too. So Jerome decided to put the Bible in words people could read and understand. Today, we know Jerome as Saint Jerome. We honor him as one of the great teachers of the Church.

? How did Jerome help other people read and learn from the Bible?

The Written Word of God

The **Bible** is a holy book. It is God's own Word to us. When we read or listen to the Word of God in the Bible, God speaks to us. In the Bible, God tells us about his great love for us.

God chose special people to write the Bible. God the Holy Spirit helped people write what God wanted to tell us. The Bible has two main parts. The first main part is the Old Testament. The second main part is the New Testament. The New Testament tells about Jesus and his **disciples**.

We are to live as disciples of Jesus. The Bible tells us to follow Jesus. We are to treat others as God wants us to treat them.

Faith Focus
What is the Bible?

Faith Vocabulary
Bible
The Bible is the written Word of God.

disciples
Disciples are people who follow and learn from someone. Disciples of Jesus follow and learn from him.

Activity

Decorate the Bible. Show that you know it is God's own Word to us.

King David

We read the story of King David in the Old Testament. King David was a musician. He wrote many prayers that were songs. These prayers are called psalms.

Songs in the Bible

The Bible is like a library. It has many books in it. All of the books tell us of God's love for us. One of those books is called the Book of Psalms.

Psalms are prayers we can sing. The Book of Psalms is in the Old Testament. There are 150 psalms in the Book of Psalms. These words from Psalm 119 sing about God's Word:

The Word of God makes people joyful.
The Word of God helps people know God.
The Word of God is true and lasts forever.

BASED ON PSALM 119:14, 130, 160

Activity

Sing this psalm to the tune "Mary Had a Little Lamb."

Pay attention to God's Word.
It brings joy,
Hope, and light,
Helping all of us to know
What is true and right.

BASED ON PSALM 119

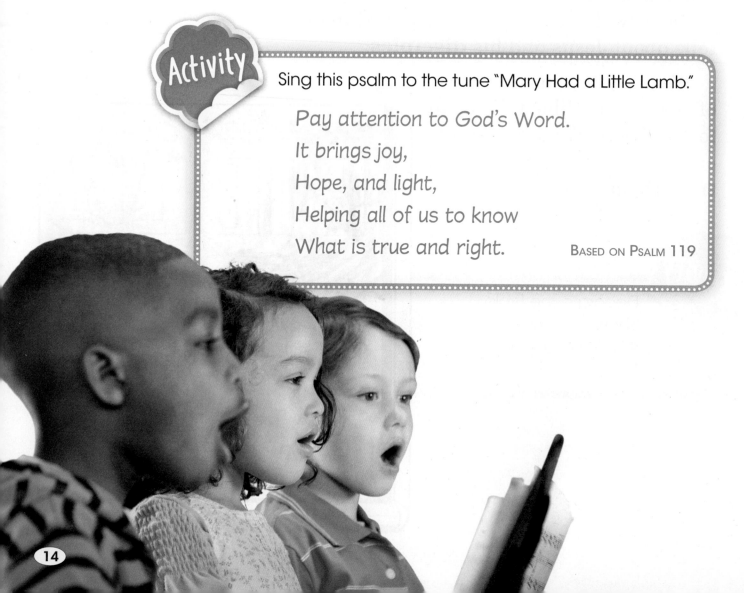

The Bible Tells Good News

The Gospels are the most important books in the Bible. The Bible has four Gospels. They are in the New Testament.

The Gospels were written by Saint Matthew, Saint Mark, Saint Luke, and Saint John. All four Gospels spread the Good News. The Good News is that God loves us very much.

Each Gospel tells what Jesus said and did. Each Gospel tells how Jesus helped people learn about God. Each Gospel tells what we must do to become Jesus' disciples.

The most important part of the Gospels is the story of Jesus' dying on the Cross and his rising from the dead.

? What is one Gospel story you know about Jesus? What does it tell you about him?

Matthew

Mark

Luke

John

I Follow Jesus

Disciples of Jesus respect others. You are a disciple of Jesus. You can pay attention to God's Word. You can tell others about Jesus. You can help people come to know more about God's great love for them.

Activity

Sharing the Good News

Write or draw a picture of one way you can tell people about Jesus. Show how you can show respect to a friend or someone in your family.

My Faith Choice

This week, I will read from the Bible. I will share with others what I read. I will

_____

_____.

Pray, "Thank you, Holy Spirit, for helping me to pay attention and learn from the Bible. Amen."

Chapter Review

Read each sentence. Draw a line through each ending that does not belong.

1. The Bible is the written
- ~~history of the world.~~
- Word of God.

2. The two main parts of the Bible are the
- ~~Psalms and the Gospels.~~
- Old Testament and the New Testament.

3. The Gospels tell us about
- ~~the creation of the world.~~
- what Jesus said and did.

A Listening Prayer

Pray together. Ask God to help you listen to his Word.

Leader O God, open our ears to hear you. Open our hearts to love you.

All **Help us pay attention to your Word.**

Leader Listen to God's Word. *(Read aloud Colossians 3:16-17.)* The word of the Lord.

All **Thanks be to God.**

Leader Let us think about what we heard God saying to us in this reading. *(Pause.)*

All **O God, we are happy to hear your Word and keep it.**

BASED ON LUKE 11:28

With My Family

This Week . . .

In Chapter 1, "The Bible," your child learned:

▶ The Bible is the written Word of God. The Old Testament and the New Testament are the two main parts of the Bible.

▶ The Holy Spirit inspired the human writers of the Bible. This means that they wrote without error what God wished to communicate.

▶ The four accounts of the Gospel are the center of the Bible.

▶ Your child also learned that paying attention shows respect.

For more about related teachings of the Church, see the *Catechism of the Catholic Church*, 101–114, and the *United States Catholic Catechism for Adults*, pages 11–32.

■ Sharing God's Word

Choose a favorite story or passage from the Gospels. Invite your child to listen and pay attention as you read the story to him or her. Afterward, invite your child to tell what she or he heard.

■ Living as Disciples

The Christian home and family is a school of discipleship. Choose one or more of the following activities to do as a family, or design a similar activity of your own:

▶ Display your family Bible in a place of prominence in your home. Gather around the Bible to read the Bible and for family prayer.

▶ Teach your child the good habit of paying attention. Paying attention is a sign of respect. Paying attention opens us to God speaking to us. Paying attention makes us aware of people in need and opens us up to reach out to them. That awareness leads us to respond—to act with charity and justice.

■ Our Spiritual Journey

Daily prayer is a vital element in the life of the Catholic family. It is one of the foundational spiritual disciplines of a disciple of Jesus. In this chapter, your child prayed and listened to Scripture. This type of prayer is called lectio divina. Learn the rhythm of lectio divina and pray this form of prayer often as a family. Read and pray together the prayer on page 17.

For more ideas on ways your family can live as disciples of Jesus, visit

www.BeMyDisciples.com

CHAPTER 2

We Know and Love God

? Who helps you read a story, play a game, or pray?

Listen to these words from the Bible. They tell us who helps us come to know God.

Help me know you, God. Teach me your

ways.   BASED ON PSALM 25:4

? Who else has helped you come to know and love God?

Hospitality

Jesus tells us to treat all people with hospitality. Hospitality helps us welcome others as God's children. It helps us treat others with dignity and respect.

The Church Follows **Jesus**

Welcome!

Mr. and Mrs. Chen are standing outside Holy Trinity Catholic Church. The sun is shining. They are smiling as they greet everyone, one by one, "Welcome! Glad to see you!"

Mr. and Mrs. Chen are ushers who greet people as they arrive for Sunday Mass at their parish.

The Chen family is very active in their parish. The Chen children go to religious education classes after school on Wednesdays. Mrs. Chen is a second-grade teacher. Mr. Chen runs the Holy Trinity Community Care Center.

They share food and clothing, books and toys, and other things with families who do not have enough money. Best of all, they treat everyone with respect. They are proud to live as joyful disciples of Jesus.

? How were the Chens good disciples of Jesus?

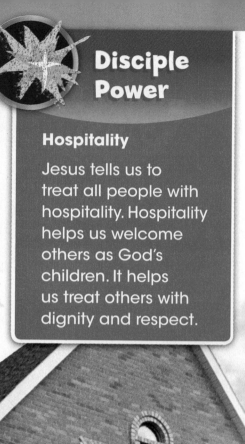

Creation Tells Us About God

The Chens help people learn about God. God's creation helps us to come to know and **believe** in him. Creation is everything that God has made. All creation helps us come to know and love God.

People are the most important part of God's creation. All people are created in the image of God. They are signs of God's love.

Our families and people in our Church help us to know God, to love him, and to serve him. But God is the one who best invites us to believe in him. God invites us to know him better and to love and serve him. God invites us to give ourselves to him with all our hearts.

Faith Focus
What are some ways God invites us to know and believe in him?

Faith Vocabulary
▶ **believe**
To believe in God means to know God and to give ourselves to him with all our hearts.

▶ **faith**
Faith is a gift from God that makes us able to believe in him.

Activity

Finish this prayer:

Thank you, God, for

Earth.

I believe that you

Love us.

Amen.

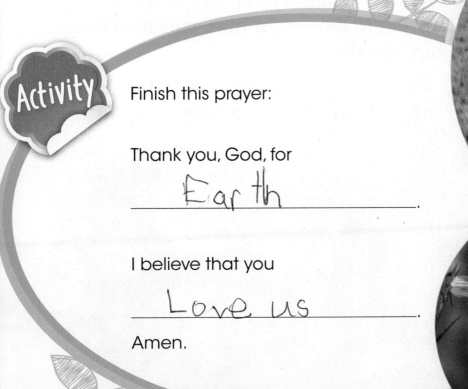

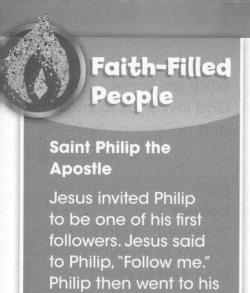

Saint Philip the Apostle

Jesus invited Philip to be one of his first followers. Jesus said to Philip, "Follow me." Philip then went to his friend Nathanael and told him about Jesus. Nathanael believed too and became a follower of Jesus.

Jesus Helps Us Know God

Jesus told us the most about God. One day a crowd of people came to Jesus. They wanted to know about God. Jesus told them that people were more important to God than everything else he created. They should believe in God with all their hearts.

Jesus said, "Look at the birds. They have all the food they need. Your Father in heaven takes care of them. You are more important to God than the birds and all the animals."

BASED ON MATTHEW 6:26

In this Bible story, Jesus invites us to have **faith** in God's loving care for us. Faith is God's gift to us. Faith makes us able to know God and to believe in what he teaches. When we say yes to God's invitation to believe in him, we show that we have faith.

? What does the Bible story tell you about God? Tell a partner.

The Church Helps Us Know God

Jesus gave us the Church. The Church is a sign of God's love in the world. The Church is the People of God who believe in Jesus Christ.

We belong to the Catholic Church. The Catholic Church goes all the way back to the time of Jesus and the Apostles. The Church helps us to know God and his love for us. The Church helps us grow in faith.

We grow in faith with the people of our Church in many ways. We pray together. We try to be kind to others. We care for God's creation. When we live our faith, we are signs of God's love for others to see.

Catholics Believe

The Parish Church

Every Catholic parish has a special name. These names, such as Holy Trinity, tell us about our faith in God. Others, such as Divine Savior Parish, tell us something specific about Jesus. Other parishes are named after Mary and the other Saints.

Activity

Circle the ways you are growing in faith. Then write another way your faith is growing.

1. I pray with others.

2. I am kind to my friends.

3. I participate during Mass.

_____

I Follow Jesus

You are a sign of God's love. You can help other people to know and believe in God by what you say and what you do.

You can practice hospitality. You can invite and welcome others to know and believe in God.

Activity

Signs of God's Love

Who can you invite to learn more about God? Write that person's name on the invitation.

You Are Invited

to Believe in God.

God Invites

_____

(friend's name)

to know and believe in him.

My Faith Choice

This week, I will show someone that I know and love God. I will

_____

_____.

Pray, "Thank you, Holy Spirit, for the gift of faith. Help me share with others how much you love them. Amen."

Chapter Review

Complete the missing letters in the sentences.

1. Faith is to k _n_ o _w_ God and to
   b _e_ l _i_ e _v_ _e_ in him with all
   our hearts.

2. The C _h_ u _r_ c _h_ helps us grow in faith.

3. Hospitality helps us treat others with
   re _s_ p _e_ c _t_.

We Believe in God!

Vocal prayers are said aloud with others.
Pray this act of faith together.

Leader   Let us pray.

Group 1   God our loving Father, all creation reminds us of your love.

All   **God, we believe in you with all our hearts.**

Group 2   Jesus, Son of God, you showed us how much God loves us.

All   **God, we believe in you with all our hearts.**

Group 3   God the Holy Spirit, you help us to know and believe in God.

All   **God, we believe in you with all our hearts.**

With My Family

This Week . . .

In Chapter 2, "We Know and Love God," your child learned:

▶ Faith is God's gift that makes us able to believe in him. God invites us to believe in him.

▶ All creation, especially our families and people in our Church, help us come to know and believe in God.

▶ Jesus revealed to us the most about God. He is the greatest sign of God's love and invites us to have faith in God.

▶ The virtue of hospitality guides us to share our faith in God with others.

For more about related teachings of the Church, see the *Catechism of the Catholic Church*, 50–67, 84–95, and 142–175, and the *United States Catholic Catechism for Adults*, pages 50–53.

■ Sharing God's Word

Read Matthew 6:26-34. Jesus invites the people to have faith in God. Or read the adaptation of the story on page 22. Talk about how your family blessings strengthen your faith in God.

■ Living as Disciples

The Christian home and family is a school of discipleship. Choose one of the following activities to do as a family, or design a similar activity of your own:

▶ Name some people who help your family come to know and believe in God. Write a note of thanks to each person on the list over the next few weeks.

▶ Identify the ways that your family lives the virtue of hospitality. Help your child grow as someone who is open and welcoming. Do this by the example of your own words and actions.

■ Our Spiritual Journey

Prayer is vital to the Christian life. Conversing with God in prayer can help us find and receive direction for living as a Catholic family. Help your child develop the habit of praying regularly. In this chapter, your child learned to pray an act of faith. Read and pray together the prayer on page 25.

For more ideas on ways your family can live as disciples of Jesus, visit **www.BeMyDisciples.com**

CHAPTER 3

The Holy Trinity

? What is something you learned recently? Who helped you learn it?

Jesus wanted us to know something very important about God. Listen to find out who Jesus said would help us. Jesus told his disciples:

I will ask the Father to send you the Holy Spirit. He will always be with you as your helper and teacher. BASED ON JOHN 14:25-26

? What did Jesus tell us about God?

Wonder

Wonder is a Gift from the Holy Spirit. It helps us see God's greatness. Wonder helps us discover more about God. It then moves us to praise him.

The Church Follows
Jesus

Many Languages!

People all around the world belong to the Catholic Church. They hear about Jesus in their own languages. They pray in their own languages.

Catholics pray the prayers of the Mass in their own languages. People who speak English begin the Mass, "In the name of the Father, and of the Son, and of the Holy Spirit. Amen."

People who speak Vietnamese pray, "Nhan danh Cha Va Con Va Thanh. Than."

When Catholics pray the Sign of the Cross, they show that they belong to God's family. They show that they believe what Jesus taught about God.

Activity

Learn to pray the Sign of the Cross in Spanish. Repeat the words below with your class. Then share it with your family.

"En el nombre del Padre, y del Hijo, y del Espíritu Santo. Amen."

En el nohm•bray del Pah•dray, ee del Ee•ho, ee del Es•peer•ee•too Sahn•toe. Amen.

God the Father

Jesus told us who God is. There is only one God who is God the Father, God the Son, and God the Holy Spirit. We call the One God in Three Persons the **Holy Trinity**. The word *trinity* means "three in one."

In the Apostles' Creed, Christians around the world pray, "I believe in God, the Father almighty, Creator of heaven and earth." God the Father is the First Person of the Holy Trinity.

God the Father created everyone and everything out of love. He created all people in his image and likeness. He created each person with a body and a **soul**. The soul is that part of each person that lives forever.

Jesus used the word *Abba* when he prayed to God the Father. The word *Abba* is the word for "father" in the language Jesus spoke. God the Father loves us and cares for us. He created us to be happy with him now and forever in Heaven.

? Who is the Holy Trinity?

Faith Focus
What did Jesus tell us about God?

Faith Vocabulary

Holy Trinity
The Holy Trinity is One God in Three Divine Persons—God the Father, God the Son, and God the Holy Spirit.

soul
Our soul is that part of us that lives forever.

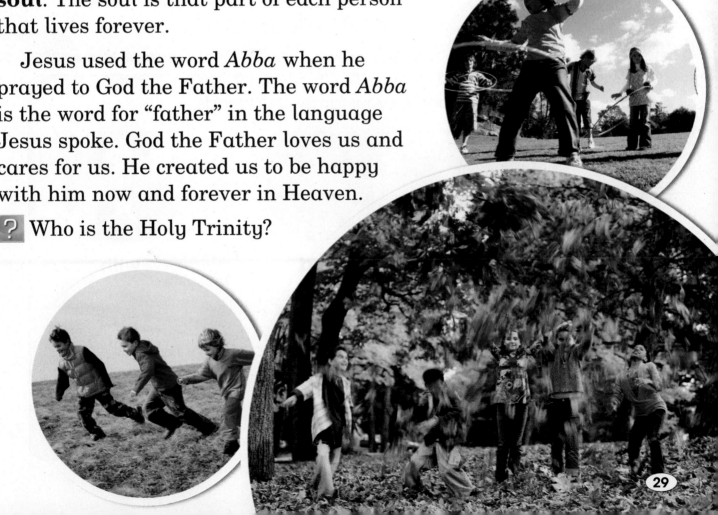

Faith-Filled People

Saint Patrick

Patrick was a bishop. He taught people about the Holy Trinity. Patrick showed people a shamrock as a symbol of the Holy Trinity. A shamrock is a plant that has three leaves connected to one stem.

God the Son

In the Apostles' Creed, we pray that we believe "in Jesus Christ, his only Son, our Lord." The word *Lord* means "God". Jesus is the Son of God who became one of us. God the Son is the Second Person of the Holy Trinity.

God the Father sent his Son to be one of us and to live with us. Jesus is the only Son of God the Father.

Jesus told us to call God our Father, too. The Bible tells us we are children of God. We are to live as children of God. Jesus taught us how to do this. He said,

"Love God with all your heart.
Love other people as much as you
love yourself."

BASED ON MATTHEW 22:37, 39

Activity

Sign this message for your family and friends.

| Love | God | with |
| all | your | heart. |

God the Holy Spirit

In the Apostles' Creed we pray, "I believe in the Holy Spirit." God the Holy Spirit is the Third Person of the Holy Trinity.

Jesus told us about the Holy Spirit. He said to his disciples,

"The Father in heaven will send you the Holy Spirit."

BASED ON LUKE 11:13

At Baptism, the priest or deacon baptizes in the name of the Father, and of the Son, and of the Holy Spirit. This shows that we share in the life of the Holy Trinity.

We first receive the gift of the Holy Spirit at Baptism. The Holy Spirit is always with us. He helps us to know, love, and serve God better. The Holy Spirit helps us to live as children of God and disciples of Jesus.

? What are three things the Holy Spirit helps us do?

I Follow Jesus

God the Holy Spirit gives you the gift of wonder. The gift of wonder helps you want to know God more. The more you know about God, the more you can tell others about God.

Activity

Telling Others About the Holy Trinity

On each leaf of the shamrock, draw or write one thing you can tell others about the Holy Trinity.

My Faith Choice

I will tell other people about the Holy Trinity this week. I will

_____.

 Pray, "Thank you, Holy Spirit, for the gift of wonder. Thank you for helping me to learn about you."

Chapter Review

Complete the sentences. Use the words in the word box.

~~Lord~~	~~One~~	~~Three~~	~~Trinity~~

1. We believe in the Holy ____Trinity____.

2. There is ____one____ God in ____three____ Divine Persons.

3. The word ____Lord____ means God.

TO HELP YOU REMEMBER

1. God is the Holy Trinity. God the Father is the First Person of the Holy Trinity.

2. God the Son is the Second Person of the Holy Trinity.

3. God the Holy Spirit is the Third Person of the Holy Trinity.

The Sign of the Cross

A ritual uses words, gestures, or actions to help us pray. Pray now using a ritual action.

Leader Come forward one at a time. Bow before the Bible. Trace a cross on your forehead, your lips, and over your heart.

All **(Come forward one at a time.)**

Leader Loving God, you are Father, Son, and Holy Spirit. Thank you for creating us.

All **Amen.**

With My Family

This Week...

In Chapter 3, "The Holy Trinity," your child learned:

▶ God is the Holy Trinity. The mystery of the Holy Trinity is the mystery of One God in Three Divine Persons: Father, Son, and Holy Spirit.

▶ We could never have come to know this wonderful truth about the identity of God on our own. We only know this about God because he has revealed this about himself in Jesus Christ.

▶ The Church's belief in the mystery of the Holy Trinity is at the heart of the Church's living faith.

▶ Wonder, one of the seven Gifts of the Holy Spirit, urges us to come to know and praise God for who he is.

For more about related teachings of the Church, see the *Catechism of the Catholic Church*, 232–260, and the *United States Catholic Catechism for Adults*, pages 51–53.

Sharing God's Word

Read together John 14:26, the promise of Jesus that the Holy Spirit would come to his disciples. Talk about how wonderful it is that Jesus revealed that there is One God, who is Father, Son, and Holy Spirit.

Living as Disciples

The Christian home and family is a school of discipleship. Choose one of the following activities to do as a family, or design a similar activity of your own:

▶ Awaken your child's awareness of the gift of wonder. Share both your curiosity and your delight in the mystery of God manifested in the world around you. Point out the many elements of God's creation that help you come to know more about him.

▶ Create a Holy Trinity banner. Display it at the entrance to your home. Use it as a reminder that God the Holy Trinity dwells in your home with your family.

Our Spiritual Journey

Praying a doxology is an ancient tradition of the Church. A doxology is a prayer giving praise and honor to God. Remind one another that all you say and do is to give glory to God. Pray the Glory Be on page 257 regularly together with your child.

For more ideas on ways your family can live as disciples of Jesus, visit **www.BeMyDisciples.com**

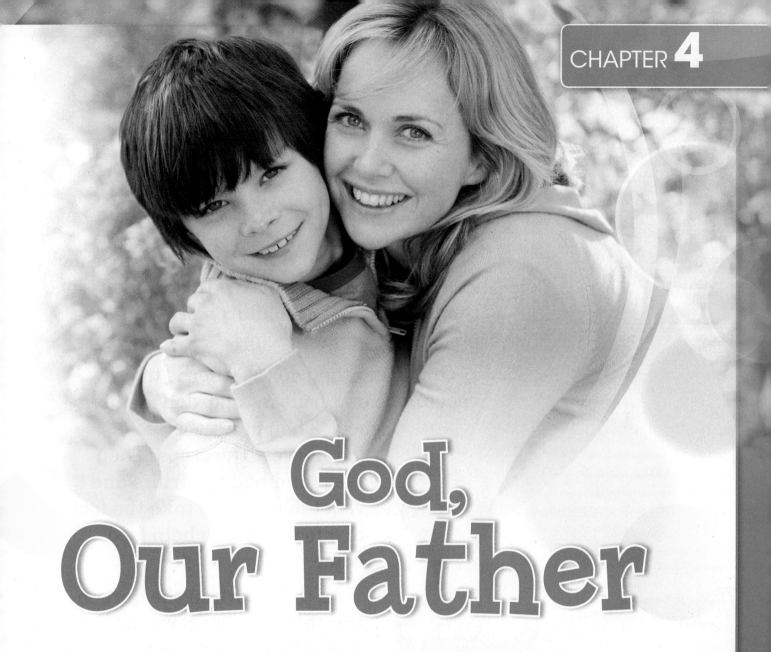

CHAPTER 4

God, Our Father

? What are some of the things parents do to show their love for their children?

Listen to what Saint John wrote about God the Father.

God our Father loves us with a wonderful love! We are so glad to be his children.

BASED ON 1 JOHN 3:1

? What are some ways God the Father shows his wonderful love for you?

Honor

When we honor others, we show respect and value them. We honor God because we are proud to be his children.

The Church Follows **Jesus**

A Garden for Others

The students at Saint Augustine's School know how much God loves them. They try their best to live as children of God. They honor God in many ways.

One thing they do together is to grow vegetables and fruit in a garden at their school. They plant the seeds and harvest the crops. They wash and bag the fruits and vegetables. They take the food to a food bank to help feed people.

As they work in the garden, the children feel close to God. They show their love for God the Creator and people when they take care of creation. They show they are proud to be children of God.

Activity

Draw yourself in this photo caring for creation.

God the Creator

You are getting to know more and more about God. God is the Father and the **Creator**. He made everyone and everything out of love and without any help. He made the creatures we can see and the angels we cannot see.

God tells us that he alone is the Creator. He tells us this in the first story of the Bible.

In the beginning, God created the heavens and the earth. He made the sun, the other stars, and the moon. He made the sky, the earth, and the sea.

God made plants, trees, and flowers. He made all the fish and the birds. He made all the animals and other creatures that live on the land. Then God created people in his image and likeness. God looked at all that he had created. He saw that it was very good.

BASED ON GENESIS 1:1, 7-12, 16, 20-21, 24-25, 27, 31

? Which part of God's creation was made in his image and likeness?

Faith Focus
Why do we call God, our Father?

Faith Vocabulary
Creator
God alone is the Creator. God made everyone and everything out of love and without any help.

almighty
God alone is almighty. This means that only God has the power to do everything good.

37

Saint Bonaventure

Bonaventure looked at creation and came to know more about God. He said that creation was like a mirror. Whenever he looked at creation, Bonaventure saw that God was good and loving. The Church celebrates his feast day on July 15.

God the Almighty

We can learn about God when we look at creation. We can see how much God loves us. We can learn that God is **almighty**. This means that only God has the power to do everything good.

God tells us that he does everything out of love. He is always good and loving. We believe in and love God the Father with all our hearts. We show God and others our trust and love for him.

Activity

Find and circle the words in the puzzle that tell about God. What does each word tell you about God?

Creator   Father   Almighty   Love   Good

C	B	G	O	O	D	R	D	G	T
A	Z	D	X	P	Q	L	M	Y	E
K	X	E	L	T	K	G	P	Z	U
L	F	A	L	M	I	G	H	T	Y
C	R	E	A	T	O	R	V	Q	N
I	K	T	Z	L	O	V	E	X	B
G	F	A	T	H	E	R	Y	Q	F

God Our Father

Jesus told us the most about God. One day, Jesus' friends asked him to teach them to pray. He taught them to pray:

Our Father in heaven,
hallowed be your name.

MATTHEW 6:9

The word *hallowed* means "very holy." We give great honor to God when we say, "hallowed be your name."

Jesus taught that God his Father is our Father. God the Father loves and cares for us. He knows what we need before we ask for it. God always does what is best for us. We are to believe in him and trust him. We are to honor him as Jesus did.

? What did Jesus teach us about God the Father?

Catholics Believe

The Lord's Prayer

The Our Father is the prayer of all Christians. It is called the Our Father because the first words of the prayer are "Our Father." Jesus our Lord gave this prayer to the Church. This is why the Our Father is also called the Lord's Prayer.

I Follow Jesus

God created everyone and everything out of love. God shares the gift of his love with you every day. You can give honor to God the Father by caring for creation.

Activity

How can your class show that you are proud to be children of God? Write or draw your ideas here.

My Faith Choice

This week, I will honor God by showing my love for all of creation. I will

_____

_____

 Pray, "Thank you, God the Holy Spirit, for helping me to honor God the Father by caring for creation. Amen."

Chapter Review

Complete the crossword puzzle.

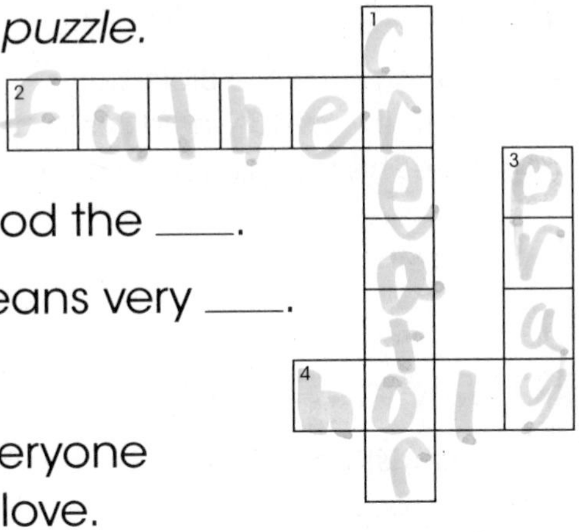

Across

2. Creation is a sign of God the ____.

4. The word *hallowed* means very ____.

Down

1. God the ____ made everyone and everything out of love.

3. Jesus taught us to ____ the Our Father.

TO HELP YOU REMEMBER

1. God is the Creator. He made everyone and everything because of his love.
2. God is almighty. He alone can do everything good.
3. Jesus taught us that God the Father is our Father.

Our Father

Christians pray the Our Father every day. Pray the Our Father together now.

Our Father, who art in heaven,
hallowed be thy name;
thy kingdom come,
thy will be done
  on earth as it is in heaven.
Give us this day our daily bread,
and forgive us our trespasses,
as we forgive those who trespass
  against us;
and lead us not into temptation,
  but deliver us from evil. Amen.

With My Family

This Week . . .

In Chapter 4, "God, Our Father," your child learned:

▶ God is the Creator of all that exists. He alone made everyone and everything out of love without any help.

▶ We call God almighty because he has the power to do everything that is good. His power is universal, loving, and merciful.

▶ God is the origin of all that exists. He loves and cares for us.

▶ We honor God the Father when we join in caring for his creation.

▶ When we honor someone, we show them the love and respect that they deserve.

For more about related teachings of the Church, see the *Catechism of the Catholic Church*, 268–274, 279–314, and 325–349, and the *United States Catholic Catechism for Adults*, pages 50–54.

▊ Sharing God's Word

Read together the Bible story in Matthew 6:9-13 where Jesus teaches his friends how to pray. Emphasize that Jesus taught us to pray the Our Father.

▊ Living as Disciples

The Christian home and family is a school of discipleship. Choose one or more of the following activities to do as a family, or design a similar activity of your own:

▶ Draw a creation mural. Write "God the Creator" at the top of the mural. Decorate the mural with pictures of things God created.

▶ By your example, help your child honor God's creation. Demonstrate how you use water, energy and food, and your treatment of living creatures. Model respect for people. Decide as a family what you can do together.

▊ Our Spiritual Journey

In the Sermon on the Mount, Jesus gave his disciples guidelines for living as his disciples. He taught them to pray the Our Father. In this chapter, your child prayed the Our Father. Pray the Our Father together as a family this week at bedtime.

For more ideas on ways your family can live as disciples of Jesus, visit **www.BeMyDisciples.com**

Unit 1 Review

A. Choose the Best Word

Complete the sentences. Color the circle next to the best choice for each sentence.

1. The _____ is One God in Three Persons.

○ Holy Trinity   ○ Holy Spirit   ○ Holy Family

2. God the Father is the _____ who made everyone and everything out of love.

○ Apostle   ○ Creator   ○ Holy Spirit

3. Jesus is the _____ Person of the Holy Trinity.

○ First   ○ Second   ○ Third

4. The part of us that lives forever is called the _____.

○ heart   ○ mind   ○ soul

5. We honor the Holy Trinity when we pray the _____.

○ Hail Mary   ○ Sign of the Cross   ○ Lord's Prayer

B. Show What You Know

Match the numbers in Column A with the letters in Column B.

Column A	Column B
____ **1.** God the Father	**a.** Savior
____ **2.** God the Son	**b.** Creator
____ **3.** God the Holy Spirit	**c.** Helper

C. Connect with Scripture

What was your favorite story about Jesus in this unit? Draw something that happened in the story. Tell your class about it.

D. Be a Disciple

1. *What Saint or holy person did you enjoy hearing about in this unit? Write the name here. Tell your class what this person did to follow Jesus.*

_____

2. *What can you do to be a good disciple of Jesus?*

_____

_____

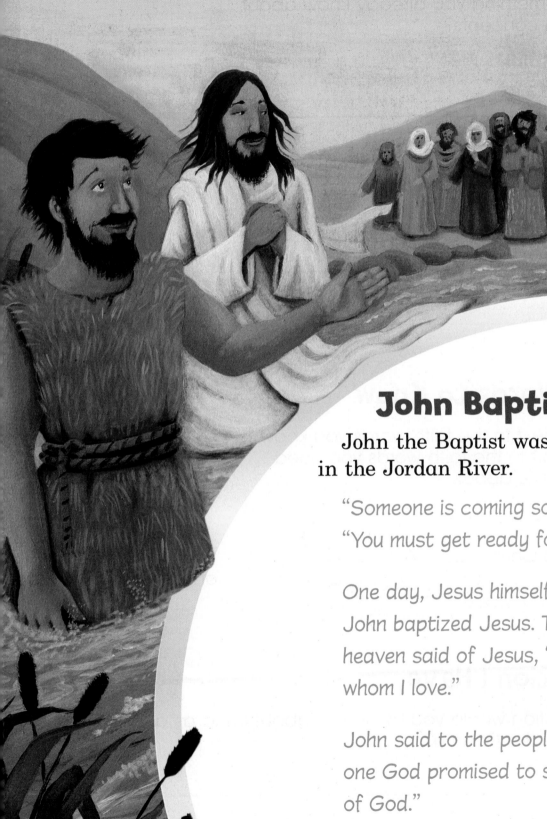

John Baptizes Jesus

John the Baptist was baptizing people in the Jordan River.

"Someone is coming soon," John said. "You must get ready for him. Sin no more."

One day, Jesus himself came to John. John baptized Jesus. Then a voice from heaven said of Jesus, "This is my Son whom I love."

John said to the people, "Look, this is the one God promised to send. He is the Son of God."

BASED ON MATTHEW 3:2-3, 13, 15, 17
AND JOHN 1:29, 34

What I Have Learned

What is something you already know about these faith concepts?

the Holy Spirit

_____

_____

the Church

_____

_____

Faith Words to Know

Put an **X** next to the faith words you know.
Put a **?** next to the faith words you need
to learn more about.

Faith Words

_____ Jesus Christ   _____ Ascension   _____ Communion
                                                     of Saints

_____ Covenant   _____ Body of Christ

A Question I Have

What question would you like to ask about living as a
member of the Church?

_____

CHAPTER 5

Jesus, Son of God

 Why is it important to keep a promise?

God made this promise to his people.
He said,

> A virgin will have a baby. They will name
> him Wonder-Counselor, God-Hero,
> Father-Forever, and Prince of Peace. The
> child will grow up and begin rebuilding
> a world of kindness and love.

BASED ON ISAIAH 7:14; 9:5-6

 Who is the child God promised?

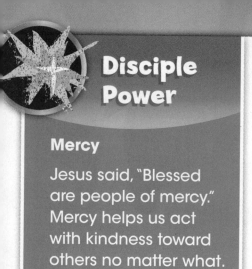
Brother Martin

Jesus is the child God promised would be born. Jesus taught us how to build a world of kindness, love, and mercy.

Martin de Porres did what Jesus asked. Martin joined a group of religious brothers and showed people the kindness and love of God.

Brother Martin cared for the sick people in Peru. He helped children who had no parents. He brought food and clothes to people in need.

All these things Brother Martin did are called Works of Mercy. When we show mercy, we share God's love with others.

Clothing DRIVE

Activity

Write how the people in the picture are building a world of mercy, kindness, and love. Write one more way that you could help.

_____

_____

_____

God's Special Promise

The Bible tells us about a very special promise God made with his people. This promise is the **Covenant**. The Covenant shows that God always loves people.

The Covenant that God and people made began at creation. Our first parents broke the promise they made to God. They sinned. We call this sin Original Sin.

God made the Covenant again with Noah and with Abraham and with Moses. God's people still sometimes broke the Covenant. When they did, God sent people to remind them to keep it.

God then promised to send someone who would make God and people friends again. God kept his promise. He sent his Son, **Jesus Christ**.

Jesus is the Second Person of the Holy Trinity who became one of us. Jesus is true God and true man.

? Why did God send his Son, Jesus?

Faith Focus
How did Jesus show that God always loves people?

Faith Vocabulary

▶ **Covenant**
The Covenant is God's promise to always love and be kind to his people.

▶ **Jesus Christ**
Jesus Christ is the Son of God. He is the Second Person of the Holy Trinity who became one of us. Jesus is true God and true man.

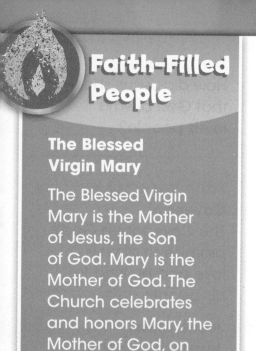

The Blessed Virgin Mary

The Blessed Virgin Mary is the Mother of Jesus, the Son of God. Mary is the Mother of God. The Church celebrates and honors Mary, the Mother of God, on January 1.

The Birth of Jesus

The Bible tells about the birth of Jesus. We call this story the Nativity.

Narrator Just before Jesus' birth, Joseph and Mary traveled to Bethlehem.

Action *Joseph knocks, and the innkeeper opens the door.*

Joseph My wife and I need a room. She is going to have a baby.

Innkeeper There are no rooms left. You may stay in the stable.

Narrator Mary and Joseph went to the stable. Jesus was born there.

BASED ON LUKE 2:4-7

The Bible tells us that angels told shepherds about the birth of Jesus. The shepherds saw him and were filled with joy! They praised God for keeping his promise.

Activity

Write the words of joy the shepherds might have said. Write your own words of joy. Give praise and thank God for sending Jesus.

Shepherds' Words

_____

My Words

_____

_____

God Cares for All People

The New Testament tells us that when Jesus grew up, he traveled from place to place. Sometimes he walked. Sometimes he rode a donkey. Sometimes he rode in a boat.

All the things Jesus said and did taught people about God's mercy and love. *Mercy* means "great kindness." Read this Bible story about God's mercy:

> Many people had followed Jesus all day long. As nighttime came, Jesus saw that the people were hungry. But there were only two fish and five loaves of bread to feed all the people. Jesus took the food, looked to heaven, and blessed the food. Then he gave the bread and the fish to his disciples and told them to give the food to the people. Everyone had enough to eat. There was even food left over.
>
> BASED ON MATTHEW 14:13-20

? How did Jesus show that God is kind to people? How are you kind to your family and friends?

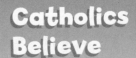

I Follow Jesus

Jesus is the greatest sign of God's love and mercy. You can be a follower of Jesus. You can be a sign of God's love and mercy, too.

Activity

Signs of God's Love and Mercy

Look at the two pictures. How are the people caring for others? Write in each bubble what the helping person might be saying.

My Faith Choice

This week, I promise to live as a sign of God's love and mercy. I will

_____

Pray, "Thank you, Holy Spirit, for helping me to live as a sign of God's love and kindness."

52

Chapter Review

Add letters to complete the words in the sentences.

1. M _____ _____ _____ is the Mother of Jesus.

2. _____ _____ s _____ _____ is the Son of God.

3. Jesus showed us God's love and

_____ _____ r _____ y.

► **TO HELP YOU REMEMBER**

1. The Covenant is a promise of God's love and mercy.

2. The birth of Jesus Christ, the Son of God, is called the Nativity.

3. Everything Jesus said and did shows us God's love and mercy.

The Angelus

The Angelus is a prayer that praises God for the gift of Jesus.

Leader   The angel spoke God's message to Mary,

Group 1   and the Holy Spirit came upon her.

All   **Hail Mary . . .**

Leader   "I am the lowly servant of the Lord:

Group 2   let it be done to me according to your word."

All   **Hail Mary . . .**

Leader   And the Word became flesh

Group 3   and lived among us.

All   **Hail Mary . . .**

With My Family

This Week...

In Chapter 5, "Jesus, Son of God," your child learned that:

▶ God and his people made the Covenant with one another.

▶ The Covenant is the promise of God's love and mercy and the promise of his people to love and serve God above all else.

▶ When Adam and Eve sinned and broke the Covenant, God promised to send someone to renew the Covenant.

▶ God fulfilled his promise by sending his Son, Jesus Christ, who became man and lived among us. Jesus Christ is true God and true man. He is the new and everlasting Covenant.

▶ The virtue of mercy helps us act with kindness toward others.

For more about related teachings of the Church, see the *Catechism of the Catholic Church*, 51–67 and 456–560, and the *United States Catholic Catechism for Adults*, pages 77–87.

■ Sharing God's Word

Read together Luke 2:1-14, about Jesus' birth. Or read the play about the Nativity on page 50. Emphasize that Jesus Christ is the Son of God. Jesus' birth is one of the most important signs that God always keeps his promise to love us.

■ We Live as Disciples

The Christian home and family is a school of discipleship. Choose one of the following activities to do as a family, or design a similar activity of your own:

▶ Share ways that your family shows mercy by acting as a living sign of God's love and kindness.

▶ Jesus told people repeatedly about God's love for them. Look around your home for something that reminds you of God's love. Talk about what it tells you about God's love.

■ Our Spiritual Journey

Devotion to Mary is a hallmark of Catholic living. Mary is an exemplar of holiness and hope and a witness to faith. Include a devotion to Mary, the Mother of God, in the spiritual journey of your family. In this chapter, your child prayed part of the Angelus. This prayer was traditionally prayed three times a day. Read and pray together the prayer on page 53.

For more ideas on ways your family can live as disciples of Jesus, visit **www.BeMyDisciples.com**

CHAPTER 6

Jesus, the Savior

? What would you give up to help a friend? Jesus told his friends,

"Love one another. You know how I have loved you. Love one another the same way. Remember, the greatest love you can show is to give up your life for your friends."

BASED ON JOHN 13:34; 15:13

? What are some ways that Jesus showed love for others?

Sacrifice

You sacrifice when you give up something because you love someone. Jesus sacrificed his life for all people. Followers of Jesus make sacrifices out of love for God and for people.

The Church Follows **Jesus**

Saint Elizabeth of Hungary

Elizabeth was born many years ago to the king and queen of the country called Hungary. Princess Elizabeth was very rich. She was also very generous. She loved Jesus. She followed Jesus' commandment to love as he loved.

Elizabeth loved the people in her country. After her husband died, she gave up everything she had out of her love for God and others. Princess Elizabeth gave away her fancy clothes, jewels, and money to help people. She gave food to people who were hungry. She cared for people who were sick.

Today we remember Princess Elizabeth as Saint Elizabeth of Hungary. We celebrate her feast on November 17.

[?] How did Saint Elizabeth show her love for Jesus and for the people of Hungary?

God Sent the Savior

God promised to send his people a savior. A savior is a person who sets people free. God the Father sent his Son, Jesus, to be the Savior of the world. God sent Jesus to save people from their sins.

Saint Matthew tells us about the announcement that God would send the Savior.

One night when Joseph was sleeping, an angel brought him a message from God. The angel said to Joseph, "Mary, your wife, will give birth to a son. You are to give him the name Jesus. He will save his people from their sins. All this will happen to fulfill God's promises." BASED ON MATTHEW 1:20-23

The name Jesus means "God saves." Jesus died on the Cross to save us from our sins.

Activity Color the name Jesus. Say a prayer thanking Jesus for his love. Share your prayer with a partner.

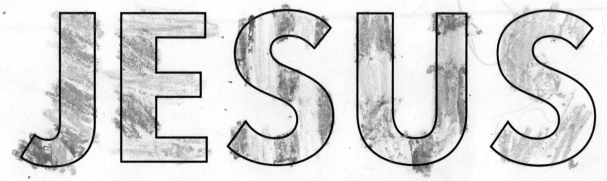

Saint Mary Magdalene

Mary Magdalene stood by the Cross of Jesus with Mary, the Mother of Jesus, and with several other disciples of Jesus. She was one of the first disciples to whom the Risen Jesus appeared. The Church celebrates her feast day on July 22.

Jesus Died on the Cross

Jesus showed his love for his Father and for all people by freely dying on the Cross. Jesus' Death on a cross is called the **Crucifixion**.

This is part of the story of what happened at the Crucifixion. Saint Luke tells us,

> On a hill near the city of Jerusalem, soldiers put Jesus to death on a cross. The name of the hill is Calvary. The sky became very dark. Jesus said, "Father, forgive them." Then Jesus died.
>
> BASED ON LUKE 23:33-34, 44, 46

Jesus' Death on the Cross is also called the Sacrifice of the Cross. Jesus sacrificed his life to save and free us from sin and death. Through Jesus' Death on the Cross, God forgives us our sins. Jesus is the Savior of the world.

Jesus has made us friends with God again. We can live forever with God in Heaven.

[?] What does the Crucifixion mean?

Jesus Is Raised to New Life

Something amazing happened three days after Jesus died and was buried in the tomb. Mary Magdalene and two other women disciples of Jesus went to the place where Jesus was buried. When they arrived there, the women saw that the body of Jesus was not there.

Two men dressed in bright white robes appeared to them and said, "Jesus is not here. He has been raised." They left the tomb and told the Apostles and others what happened. Peter and the others did not believe them. They rushed to the tomb to see for themselves if what the women disciples said was true.

BASED ON LUKE 24:4, 6, 9, 11-12

Jesus rose from the dead to new life. We call this the **Resurrection**.

We too shall live after we die. All the faithful friends of Jesus will live in happiness forever in Heaven.

The Crucifix

The crucifix is a cross with an image of Jesus on it. The crucifix is a sign of God's love and mercy. Many families have a crucifix in their homes. Some Christians wear a crucifix on a chain around their neck to show their love for Jesus. There is always a crucifix placed near the altar in church.

Activity

Connect the dots to discover a word that means "Praise God."

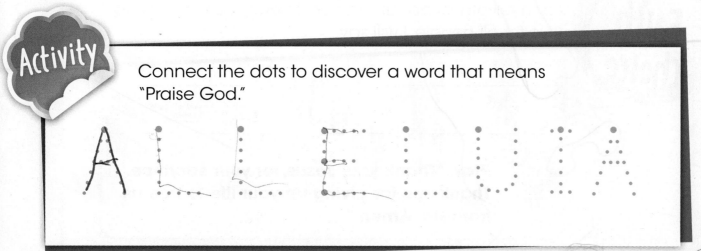

ALLELUIA

I Follow Jesus

Jesus is the Savior of all people. He sacrificed his life out of love for his Father and for all people. The Holy Spirit invites you to share this good news with everyone.

Activity

Alleluia! Praise God!

Decorate this bookmark with colors and pictures that help you remember Jesus is the Savior of the world.

Save us, Savior of the world,
for by your Cross and Resurrection
you have set us free.

Alleluia!

MEMORIAL ACCLAMATION C, *ROMAN MISSAL*

My Faith choice

I can tell others about the good news of Jesus' saving love for all people. I will say:

_____

_____.

Pray, "Thank you, Jesus, for your sacrifice. Thank you for giving up your life to free us from sin. Amen."

Chapter Review

Use the words in the box to complete the sentences.

Savior	Resurrection	Crucifixion

1. God the Father raising Jesus to new life is

   called the _____.

2. God the Father sent Jesus to be the

   _____.

3. Jesus' Death on a cross is called the

   _____.

TO HELP YOU REMEMBER

1. Jesus Christ is the Savior of the world.

2. Jesus sacrificed his life on a cross to save all people from their sins.

3. God the Father raised his Son, Jesus, from death to new life.

Praise God

Acclamations are prayers of praise. We pray acclamations to praise God for all the wonderful things he has done. Pray this acclamation that we pray aloud or sing at Mass.

Leader Let us proclaim the mystery of faith.

All **Save us, Savior of the world, for by your Cross and Resurrection you have set us free.**

MEMORIAL ACCLAMATION C, *ROMAN MISSAL*

With My Family

This Week . . .

In Chapter 6, "Jesus, the Savior," your child learned:

▶ Salvation flows from God's initiative of love and mercy. God the Father sent his Son, Jesus, who freely chose to sacrifice his life on a cross to free all people from sin.

▶ Three days after his Death and burial, Jesus rose from the dead to a new and glorified life. We call this event the Resurrection.

▶ We too shall live after we die. God invites us to live an eternal life of happiness.

▶ Jesus sacrificed his life for all people. Followers of Jesus make sacrifices out of love for God and for people.

For more about related teachings of the Church, see the *Catechism of the Catholic Church*, 422–451, 456–478, 599-655, and the *United States Catholic Catechism for Adults*, pages 91–98.

■ Sharing God's Word

Read the Bible story about Jesus' dying on the Cross and his rising from the dead. Emphasize that the Death and Resurrection of Jesus are the greatest signs of God's love for people.

■ We Live as Disciples

The Christian home and family is a school of discipleship. Choose one of the following activities to do as a family, or design a similar activity of your own:

▶ The crucifix reminds us of God's love for us. Display a crucifix in your home. Gather around it and talk about God's love for your family.

▶ Help your child practice making sacrifices. Offer him or her opportunities to choose others over himself or herself. For example, if your child gets an allowance, suggest ways he or she can give a portion to help the hungry.

■ Our Spiritual Journey

The Sacrifice of the Cross is the greatest expression of God's love for people. Christians are people of sacrifice. In this chapter, your child learned to pray a Memorial Acclamation used at Mass. Read and pray together the prayer on page 61.

For more ideas on ways your family can live as disciples of Jesus, visit **www.BeMyDisciples.com**

CHAPTER 7

The Holy Spirit

? What is the best gift someone ever gave you?

Saint Paul tells us,

God loves you very much. God sends you the Holy Spirit. The Holy Spirit gives special spiritual gifts to each person. The Holy Spirit wants us to use our gifts to help and serve others. BASED ON 1 CORINTHIANS 12:4-7

? What special gifts do you have that help and serve others?

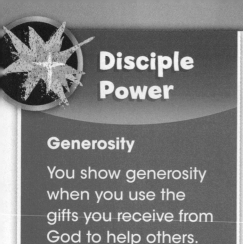

Generosity

You show generosity when you use the gifts you receive from God to help others.

The Church Follows **Jesus**

Kids' Kitchen

We all receive blessings and gifts from the Holy Spirit. Even second graders get these gifts! One of these gifts is the gift of generosity.

Sagen was in second grade. She saw that some children ate free lunches at school. She wondered, "What do they do during the summer? Do they get to eat lunch every day? How can I help?"

Sagen went to Sam who was in charge of the soup kitchen in her parish. Sam helped Sagen organize her own kitchen for kids. She called it Kids' Kitchen.

The word spread about Kids' Kitchen. Many people were donating food. Kids' Kitchen was able to help more and more kids.

? How do you see people in your parish being generous?

The Gift of the Holy Spirit

After the Resurrection, Jesus made a special promise to his disciples. He said,

I am sending the promise of my Father to you. It is the gift of the Holy Spirit.

BASED ON LUKE 24:49

The Holy Spirit is the Third Person of the Holy Trinity.

Jesus made this promise after the Resurrection, just before he returned to his Father in Heaven. We call the return of the Risen Jesus to his Father in Heaven the **Ascension**.

Faith Focus
What does the New Testament tell us about the Holy Spirit?

Faith Vocabulary
Ascension
The Ascension is the return of the Risen Jesus to his Father in Heaven forty days after the Resurrection.

Pentecost
Pentecost is the day the Holy Spirit came to the disciples of Jesus fifty days after the Resurrection.

Activity

Decorate this postcard. Share Jesus' promise with your family and friends.

Saint Luke the Evangelist

Luke sometimes traveled from place to place with Saint Paul. Together they preached the Gospel. They told people all about Jesus. Saint Luke is one of the four Evangelists, or "tellers of the Gospel."

Pentecost

The promise of the Holy Spirit came true fifty days after the Resurrection. The day that the Holy Spirit came to the Apostles is called **Pentecost**. This is what Saint Luke tells us happened:

After Jesus returned to his Father, the disciples and Mary, the mother of Jesus, were praying together in a room. Suddenly, a big sound filled the house. It was the sound of a strong wind. Small flames settled over each disciple's head. The disciples were all filled with the Holy Spirit. Peter and the disciples then left the house. They went to tell others about Jesus.

BASED ON ACTS OF THE APOSTLES 2:1-6

We first receive the gift of the Holy Spirit at Baptism. The Holy Spirit is always with us. He gives us special gifts to live as followers of Jesus. The Holy Spirit helps us tell others about Jesus as Peter did.

❓ What is one thing you want to tell someone about Jesus?

The Holy Spirit Is Always with Us

The Holy Spirit is the helper and teacher Jesus sent to us. The Holy Spirit helps us to believe and trust in God the Father and in Jesus Christ.

The Holy Spirit helps and teaches us to pray. He helps us to pray the way Jesus taught us. We pray to God our Father. We tell God the Father what is in our thoughts and in our hearts.

We ask the Holy Spirit to teach us and help us to live as children of God. We ask the Holy Spirit to teach us and help us to live as followers of Jesus. The Holy Spirit always helps us.

Gifts of the Holy Spirit

The Holy Spirit blesses us with spiritual gifts. These gifts help us to follow Jesus and to live as children of God.

Activity

Write a short prayer to the Holy Spirit. Use your own words.

Come, Holy Spirit, **help** me to

_____

_____.

Come, Holy Spirit, **teach** me to

_____

_____.

I Follow Jesus

The Holy Spirit gives you gifts. These gifts are sometimes called talents. Talents help us to do good things. They help you to know God's love. Generosity helps you use those gifts to help others.

Activity

Sharing the Gift of God's Love

A flame of fire reminds us of the Holy Spirit. Think of your talents. In the flame, show how you use one talent you have to help others.

My Faith Choice

This week, I will be generous. I will use my talents. I will share the gift of God's love with other people.

I will

_____

_____.

Pray, "Thank you, Holy Spirit for helping me to use my talents to help others. Amen."

Chapter Review

Match each word with its correct meaning.

Words

_____ **1.** Pentecost

_____ **2.** Ascension

_____ **3.** Jesus

_____ **4.** Holy Spirit

Meanings

a. the One who asked the Father to send the Holy Spirit

b. the day the work of the Church began

c. the Third Person of the Holy Trinity

d. the return of the Risen Jesus to his Father in Heaven

Come, Holy Spirit

Leader   Let us pray to the Holy Spirit.

All   **Come, Holy Spirit,**

Group 1   fill the hearts of your faithful, and kindle in them the fire of your love.

All   **Come, Holy Spirit,**

Group 2   send forth your Spirit and they shall be created.

Group 3   And you will renew the face of the Earth.

All   **Amen.**

With My Family

This Week . . .

In Chapter 7, "The Holy Spirit," your child learned that:

▶ The Holy Spirit is the Third Person of the Holy Trinity.

▶ The Father and the Son sent the Holy Spirit to be our helper and teacher.

▶ The Holy Spirit is the source of all the Church does.

▶ The Holy Spirit helps us to learn and to live what Jesus taught.

▶ The Holy Spirit helps all the baptized to pray and to live as children of God and followers of Christ.

▶ When we practice the virtue of generosity, we show that we are thankful for the gifts we receive from God.

For more about related teachings of the Church, see the *Catechism of the Catholic Church*, 687–741, and the United States *Catholic Catechism for Adults*, pages 102–108.

■ Sharing God's Word

Read Acts of the Apostles 2:1-11, 22 about the coming of the Holy Spirit on Pentecost. Or read the adaptation of the story on page 66. Emphasize that the Holy Spirit came to the disciples on Pentecost to help them do the work that Jesus gave them, namely, to tell the world about Jesus and make disciples of people. Share that the Holy Spirit is always with your family to teach and help you to do the same.

■ We Live as Disciples

The Christian home and family is a school of discipleship. Choose one of the following activities to do as a family, or design a similar activity of your own:

▶ Pray to the Holy Spirit before meals or bedtime this week. Use the prayer on page 69. Talk about how your family can tell others about Jesus.

▶ Help your child grow in generosity. Before your child will receive gifts, such as birthday gifts, invite him or her to give something else away. After giving, remind your child that disciples are generous with others.

■ Our Spiritual Journey

Almsgiving is sharing our material and spiritual blessings because of our love for God and for people. Almsgiving is an expression of generosity which flows from one's gratitude to God. Praise and thank God, both in words and deeds, for his blessings.

For more ideas on ways your family can live as disciples of Jesus, visit **www.BeMyDisciples.com**

CHAPTER 8

The Church

? To which communities do you belong?

The Church is a community. Saint Luke tells us,

> The followers of Jesus shared everything with one another. They prayed and broke bread together. They praised God and learned more about what Jesus taught. Others saw how they loved one another. Every day more people joined the Church.
>
> BASED ON ACTS OF THE APOSTLES 2:42-47

? What can you do with other members of the Church?

Goodness

Goodness is a sign that we are living our Baptism. When we are good to people, we show that we know they are children of God. When we are good to people, we honor God.

Father Augustus Tolton

Augustus' family was very poor. He and his family had escaped from slavery. They lived when Black children were not allowed to go to the same school as other children. Augustus grew up knowing God wanted him to become a priest. He became the first Black priest in the United States of America.

Priests do special work in the Church. They lead the members of the Church in worship. They teach them to live as Christ taught. They help them understand the Word of God.

? What is the name of your pastor? What kinds of work does he do with the people of your parish?

Names for the Church

God sent Jesus to all people. Jesus told the Apostles,

"Make all people my disciples. Baptize them and teach them all I taught you."

BASED ON MATTHEW 28:19-20

The Holy Spirit invites all people from every race and nation to become disciples of Jesus. The Church is the new People of God.

We become members of the Church at Baptism. God's people in the Catholic Church share the same faith and Sacraments. We are led by the Pope and the bishops. They take the place of the Apostles in the Church today.

Faith Focus
What is the Church?

Faith Vocabulary
Body of Christ
The Church is the Body of Christ. Jesus Christ is the Head of the Church. All the baptized are members of the Church.

Communion of Saints
The Church is the Communion of Saints. The Church is the unity of all the faithful followers of Jesus on Earth and those in Heaven.

Activity Find out the name of your bishop or archbishop. Write a prayer for him. Tell him you are praying for him.

_____

_____

_____

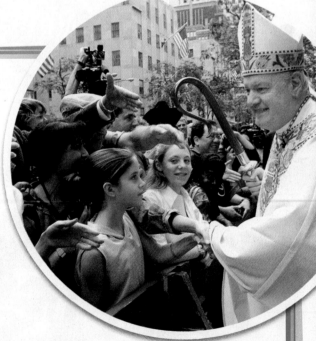

Faith-Filled People

The Faithful

The members of the Church are called the faithful. Some members of the Church are bishops, priests, and deacons. Others are religious brothers and sisters. Others are married or single men and women.

The Body of Christ

Saint Paul describes the Church as the **Body of Christ**. He wrote,

We are Christ's Body. Each of us are its parts.

BASED ON 1 CORINTHIANS 12:13

The image of the Body of Christ helps us to understand what the Church is like. The Church is the one Body of Christ. Jesus is the Head. The baptized are the Body.

All the parts of your body make up one body. Every part of your body has something different and important to do.

We all have something different and important to do. The Holy Spirit gives us the grace to live as followers of Jesus.

Activity

Look at each picture. Next to the number for each picture, write how the people are living as followers of Jesus.

1. _____

_____

2. _____

_____

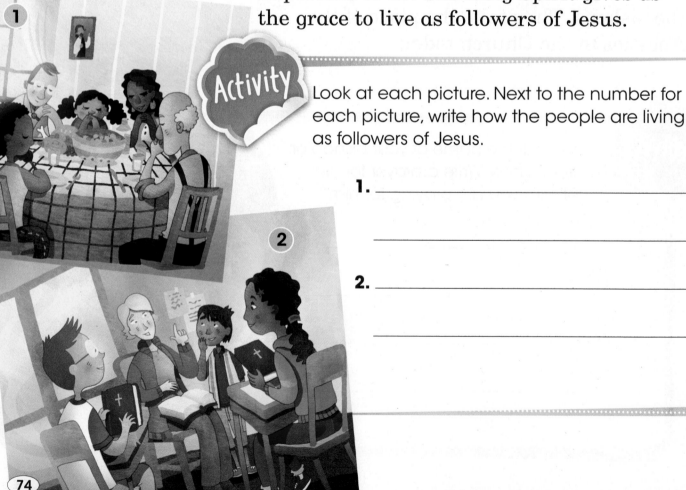

The Communion of Saints

The Church is the **Communion of Saints**, all the faithful people of God. The Church includes all the faithful followers of Jesus who live on Earth and those in Heaven.

The Church names some people who have died "Saints." The Saints live in Heaven. They are with Mary and the angels praising God with their whole hearts.

Mother of the Church

Mary is the greatest Saint. She is the Mother of God. Jesus told us that Mary is our mother. Mary is the Mother of the Church.

The Church honors Mary and the other Saints in many ways. This means that we have a special love for Mary and all the Saints who now live with God in Heaven.

The Church names certain days to honor them. We pray to Mary and the Saints. We have images of Mary and the other Saints to help us to love God and other people with our whole heart.

❓ Who is your favorite Saint? Why?

ELIZABETH ANN SETON

ELIZABETH OF PORTUGAL

ANDRE BESSETTE

I Follow Jesus

You are a member of the Body of Christ, the Church. You are a child of God. You can be good to others by helping them.

Activity

Sharing Your Faith

Think of how the Holy Spirit helps you live as a member of the Church. Write or draw something you can do with others in the Church.

My Faith Choice

This week, I will show goodness by working together with my Church to help others. I will

_____

_____

 Pray, "Saints of God, pray for me and my family. Amen."

Chapter Review

Color the box to mark the sentences that are true.

☐ Jesus gave us the Church.

☐ The Holy Spirit invites all people to become disciples of Jesus.

☐ Jesus Christ is the Head of the Church.

☐ Augustus Tolton is the greatest Saint of the Church.

▶ **TO HELP YOU REMEMBER**

1. The Church is the People of God who follow Jesus Christ.

2. The Church is the Body of Christ.

3. The Church is the Communion of Saints.

A Litany of Saints

Pray this litany with your class.

Leader   Holy Mary, Mother of God,

All   **pray for us.**

Leader   Saint Joseph,

All   **pray for us.**

Leader   Saint Elizabeth of Hungary,

All   **pray for us.**

Leader   Saint Luke the Evangelist,

All   **pray for us.**

Leader   All holy men and women,

All   **pray for us.**

With My Family

This Week . . .

In Chapter 8, "The Church," your child learned:

▶ The Church is the community of the faithful followers of Jesus.

▶ The Church is the People of God, the Body of Christ, and the Communion of Saints. Mary is the greatest Saint and Mother of the Church.

▶ All of the baptized have important roles in the work of the Church.

▶ As members of the Church, we are one in Christ. With the Holy Spirit, we can show goodness to one another. We support, care for, and show respect for one another as Jesus taught.

For more about related teachings of the Church, see the *Catechism of the Catholic Church,* 751–776, 781–801, and 874–983, and the *United States Catholic Catechism for Adults,* pages 111–147.

■ Sharing God's Word

Read together Matthew 28:19-20 about Jesus giving the Apostles the mission to make disciples of all people. Or read the adaptation of the passage on page 73. This mission is called evangelization. It is the primary work of the Church. Emphasize that the Church today continues the work Jesus gave to the first disciples.

■ We Live as Disciples

The Christian home and family is a school of discipleship. Choose one of the following activities to do as a family, or design a similar activity of your own:

▶ Talk about the many ways your family is already taking part in the work of the Church.

▶ Goodness is one of the twelve Fruits of the Holy Spirit. When we cooperate with the Holy Spirit, we are good to others. As a family, become more involved in your parish's outreach ministries to show the goodness of God to others. Look to your family's special gifts and then decide on ways you can be good to others.

■ Our Spiritual Journey

Joined to Christ and all the members of the Church at Baptism, we are strengthened and made stronger with Christ and with all the Saints in the celebration and reception of the Eucharist. Take part in the Eucharist frequently. Your child prayed part of the Litany of the Saints. Read and pray together the prayer on page 77. Add the names of your favorite Saints.

For more ideas on ways your family can live as disciples of Jesus, visit **www.BeMyDisciples.com**

Unit 2 Review

A. Choose the Best Word

Fill in the blanks to complete each of the sentences.
Use the words from the word bank.

Pentecost	covenant	People of God
Baptism	Crucifixion	

1. God made a solemn _____ with his people.

2. We call Jesus' dying on the Cross the

   _____.

3. God sent the Holy Spirit on the day of

   _____.

4. We first receive the Holy Spirit in the Sacrament

   of _____.

5. The Church is also called the _____.

B. Show What You Know

Match the items in Column A with those in Column B.

Column A

1. Communion of Saints

2. The faithful

3. the Resurrection

4. the Crucifixion

5. mercy

Column B

A. The virtue that helps us to act with kindness toward others no matter what

B. God the Father raising Jesus from the dead to new life

C. The unity of all the faithful followers of Jesus on Earth and those who have died

D. What members of the Church are called

E. What we call Jesus' dying on the Cross

C. Connect with Scripture

What was your favorite story about Jesus in this unit? Draw something that happened in the story. Tell your class about it.

D. Be a Disciple

1. *What Saint or holy person did you enjoy hearing about in this unit? Write the name here. Tell your class what this person did to follow Jesus.*

_____

2. *What can you do to be a good disciple of Jesus?*

_____

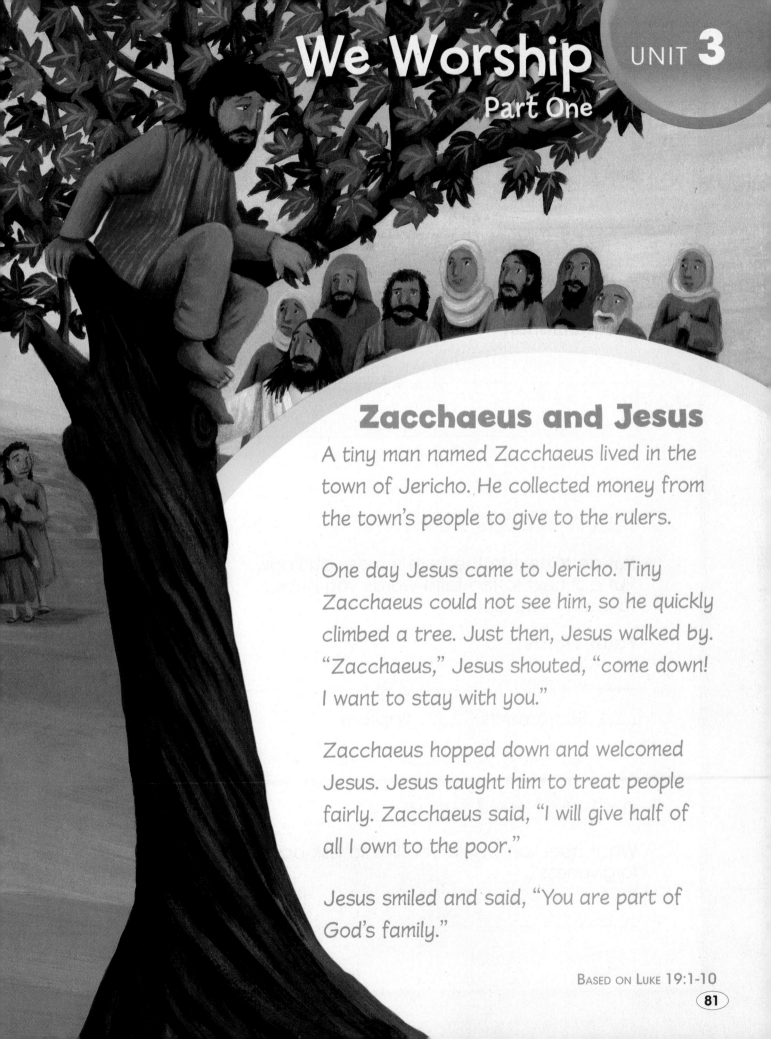

Zacchaeus and Jesus

A tiny man named Zacchaeus lived in the town of Jericho. He collected money from the town's people to give to the rulers.

One day Jesus came to Jericho. Tiny Zacchaeus could not see him, so he quickly climbed a tree. Just then, Jesus walked by. "Zacchaeus," Jesus shouted, "come down! I want to stay with you."

Zacchaeus hopped down and welcomed Jesus. Jesus taught him to treat people fairly. Zacchaeus said, "I will give half of all I own to the poor."

Jesus smiled and said, "You are part of God's family."

BASED ON LUKE 19:1-10

What I Have Learned

What is something you already know about these faith concepts?

sin

_____

_____

reconciliation

_____

_____

Faith Words to Know

Put an **X** next to the faith words you know. Put a **?** next to the faith words you need to learn more about.

Faith Words

____ worship   ____ grace   ____ Confirmation

____ Sacraments   ____ Baptism

A Question I Have

What question would you like to ask about forgiveness?

_____

CHAPTER 9

We Celebrate God's Love

? What is your favorite celebration?

The Holy Family celebrated God's love together. Listen to one of the prayers they prayed.

Shout with joy to God.

Give honor, praise, and thanks to God.

Celebrate God's love with gladness.

Sing God a song of joy. BASED ON PSALM 100:1-2

? What are some things you say or do when you celebrate God's love with your parish family?

Piety

Piety is a Gift of the Holy Spirit. Piety is the love we have for God. That love makes us want to worship and give God thanks and praise.

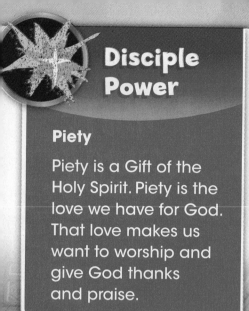

The Church Follows **Jesus**

Saint John XXIII

Saint John XXIII wanted all Catholics to celebrate God's love in the Mass. He wanted everyone to love and take part in the Mass.

Many years ago, Pope John XXIII called a meeting of all the bishops in the world. They worked together to make changes to some of the ways we celebrate the Mass.

The bishops worked together to make sure everyone could understand the words. They wanted to make sure that everyone could worship God at Mass in his or her own language.

Today we continue to celebrate Mass with renewed love for God. The words and actions we say and do at Mass help us worship God with thanks and praise.

? Which words and actions at Mass do you enjoy?

We Worship God

Jesus used words and actions to show God's love for us. One time, Jairus came to Jesus. Jairus was a religious leader who had great faith in God.

Jairus asked Jesus to help his daughter who was very sick. Read what happened next:

Jesus and his disciples followed Jairus to his house. Jesus entered the house and went over to the daughter of Jairus. Jesus took her by the hand and said, "Little girl, I say to you, arise!" The girl got up immediately and walked around.   BASED ON MARK 5:22-24, 38, 41-42

After this, more people came to believe in Jesus. His words and actions helped them believe that he is the Son of God.

Faith Focus
How does the Church worship God?

Faith Vocabulary
worship
Worship means to honor and love God above all else.

Sacraments
The Sacraments are the seven signs of God's love for us that Jesus gave the Church. We share in God's love when we celebrate the Sacraments.

Activity

With your classmates, create a skit that shows the words and actions of Jesus in this Gospel story. In your skit, show how Jesus helped others believe that he is the Son of God.

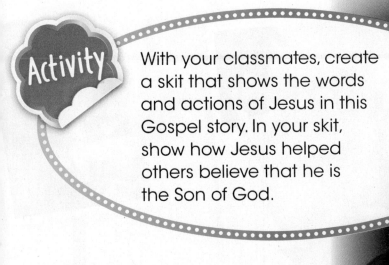

Saint Mark

Saint Mark is one of the four Evangelists. He wrote one of the four Gospels in the New Testament. In Mark's Gospel, we read about the words and actions of Jesus. The Church celebrates the feast day of Saint Mark the Evangelist on April 25.

We Praise God

God loves us very much. One way we show our love for God is to **worship** him. To worship God means to honor and love God above all else.

The Church uses words and actions in the Mass to worship God. They tell God we believe in him, hope in him, and love him.

All the words and actions we use in the Mass show that God is sharing his love with us. We use them to celebrate the **Sacraments**. The Sacraments help us to give thanks and praise to God for all he has done for us.

When we worship God, we listen to God. We give adoration to God and praise him. We pray aloud and we sing. We stand and sit and walk in procession.

Activity

Which of these pictures do you recognize as celebrations of the Church? What is happening in each picture? Tell a partner.

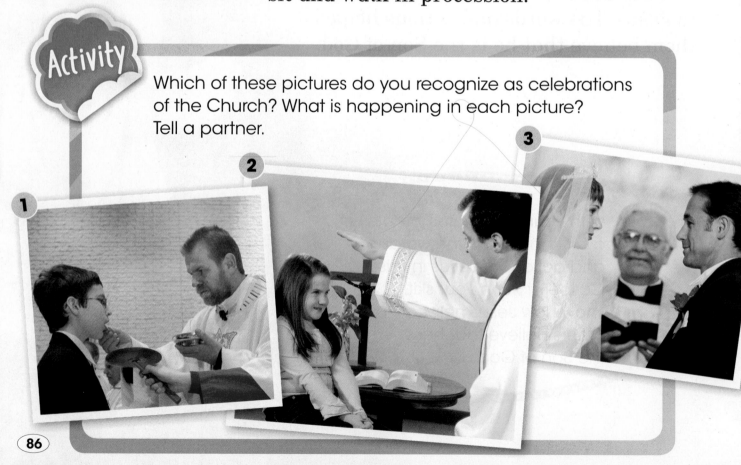

The Seven Sacraments

Jesus gave the Church a special way to worship. He gave the Church the Seven Sacraments.

The Seven Sacraments are signs of God's love for us. Jesus is present with us when we celebrate the Sacraments. The Holy Spirit helps us to celebrate the Sacraments. When we celebrate the Sacraments, we share in God's love.

Catholics Believe

Sacramentals

The Church uses objects, blessings, words, and actions to help us worship God. These are called sacramentals. Holy water is one of these objects.

Activity

Place a ✔ in the box next to the Sacraments you have received or have seen others receive. Tell about which ones you remember.

☑ **Baptism**
We are joined to Jesus and become a part of his Church.

☑ **Confirmation**
The Holy Spirit helps us to live as children of God.

☑ **The Eucharist**
We receive the Body and Blood of Jesus.

☑ **Penance and Reconciliation**
We receive God's gift of forgiveness and mercy.

☑ **Anointing of the Sick**
We receive God's healing strength when we are seriously sick or dying.

☑ **Holy Orders**
A baptized man is called by God to serve the Church as a bishop, priest, or deacon.

☑ **Matrimony**
A baptized man and a baptized woman make a lifelong promise to love and respect each other.

I Follow Jesus

The words and actions of the Sacraments are signs of God's love. Your words and actions can help people believe and trust in God's love. The Holy Spirit's gift of piety helps you to be a sign of God's love.

Activity

Praying with Actions

You can use many different actions when you pray. Finish each line of the prayer. Pray your prayer with the actions.

With hands outstretched,
I ask you, God, for

_____.

With folded hands,
I praise you, God, for

_____.

With head bowed,
I thank you, God, for

_____.

With hands raised high,
I show my love for you, O God! Amen.

My Faith Choice

This week, I will pray using both words and actions.

I will say my prayer

☐ in the morning.   ☐ after school.

☐ at dinnertime.   ☐ at bedtime.

Pray, "O Holy Spirit, let all my words and actions give praise and glory to God. Amen."

Chapter Review

Complete the sentences, using the words below.

Sacraments	actions	love

1. The words and actions of Jesus helped people

   to know God's _____.

2. We share in God's love when we celebrate the

   _____.

3. The Church uses words and _____
   to worship God.

Thank You, God

Gestures help us pray. Kneeling is one gesture we can use. It shows that we honor God.

Leader   Let us kneel before the crucifix and pray together as God's family.

All   **We love you, God.**

Leader   We are your children, God.

All   **Thank you, God, for your blessings. Amen.**

With My Family

This Week . . .

In Chapter 9, "We Celebrate God's Love," your child learned:

▶ The Church comes together to worship God.

▶ The words and actions of Jesus helped people come to believe in God and in his love for us.

▶ Through the celebration of the Sacraments, we worship God, and we are made sharers in the life and love of God.

▶ The Church uses special words and actions to celebrate the Sacraments.

▶ The virtue of piety, a special gift of the Holy Spirit, strengthens our desire to worship God.

For more about related teachings of the Church, see *Catechism of the Catholic Church*, 1066–1186, and the *United States Catholic Catechism for Adults*, pages 168–169 and 295–298.

■ Sharing God's Word

Read together Mark 5:41-42, Jesus healing the daughter of Jairus. Or read the adaptation of the story on page 85. Emphasize that Jesus healed people to show them God's love. Name and talk about some of the words and actions of your family that are signs of God's love.

■ We Live as Disciples

The Christian home and family is a school of discipleship. Choose one of the following activities to do as a family or design a similar activity of your own.

▶ Talk about which Sacraments each family member has received. Which words and actions do you remember from the celebration of each Sacrament? Discuss the meanings of those words and actions.

▶ Body language and gestures help us pray. This week hold hands when you pray as a family. Remember that you all belong to God's family as well as to your family.

■ Our Spiritual Journey

Our spiritual journey is marked by signposts. Participation in the Sacraments is vital and essential to the Christian life, in particular, participation in Mass and frequent reception of Holy Communion. Help your children learn to pray silently after Holy Communion, thanking God for his blessings in their own words.

For more ideas on ways your family can live as disciples of Jesus, visit **www.BeMyDisciples.com**

CHAPTER 10

Our Church Welcomes Us

? Who are your friends? How did you become friends?

Saint Paul wrote many letters to Jesus' followers. Listen to what he wrote in this letter.

> You have been baptized in Christ.
> It does not matter where you come from.
> It does not matter whether you are a boy
> or a girl, or a man or a woman. By
> Baptism, you are all friends of Jesus.

> BASED ON GALATIANS 3:26-28

? How do you show others that you are a friend of Jesus?

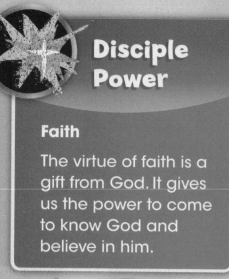
Faith

The virtue of faith is a gift from God. It gives us the power to come to know God and believe in him.

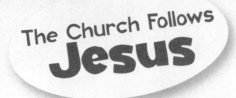

The Church Follows **Jesus**

Saint Kateri

Kateri Tekakwitha was the daughter of a Native American Mohawk warrior chief. When Kateri was only four years old, her parents died from a terrible sickness. The same sickness left Kateri almost blind and with marks and scars on her face.

One day, a priest visited her village. He told everyone that they could become followers of Jesus. Kateri learned more and more about Jesus. Then she said she wanted to be baptized. She became a follower of Jesus, a member of the Church.

Kateri prayed to God every day. She helped people in need. Even when others treated her badly, she was thankful for her faith.

Kateri helped other Native Americans become part of the Catholic Church. She showed them how to be followers of Jesus.

❓ How did Kateri show her faith in God?

Sacrament of Baptism

You learned about the Sacraments in the last chapter. **Baptism** is the first Sacrament we celebrate. The Church often celebrates Baptism during Mass.

This is what happens to us at our Baptism. We are joined to Christ. We celebrate that we are followers of Jesus. We are welcomed into the Church.

We are given the gift of the Holy Spirit. We are given a special gift called sanctifying **grace**. God shares his life with us. We are called to live a holy life.

We become adopted sons and daughters of God. We are to love God and our neighbors as Jesus taught.

Faith Vocabulary

Baptism
Baptism is the Sacrament that joins us to Christ and makes us members of the Church. We receive the gift of the Holy Spirit and become adopted sons and daughters of God.

grace
Grace is the gift of God sharing his life with us and helping us live as his children.

Activity

Finish this prayer. Pray it quietly in your heart.

Dear God our Father,

When I was baptized, I received the

Holy Spirit. I became

a member of the _Church_.

Help me always to follow your

Son, _~~Holy~~ Jesus_. Amen.

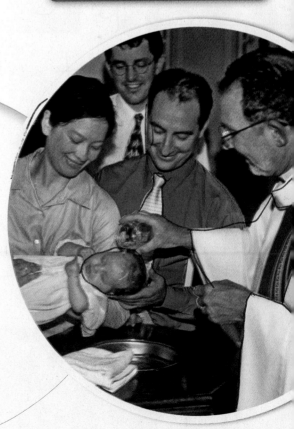

As a young man, Paul hated Christians. One day, the Risen Christ appeared to him and changed his life. Paul was baptized and became a friend of Jesus. Paul traveled everywhere to tell everyone about Jesus. He welcomed many people into the Church.

Welcome to the Church

The Bible tells us about the Baptism of a man named Cornelius and his family.

Cornelius was a soldier in the Roman army. One day he asked Peter the Apostle to tell him about Jesus.

Peter told him all about how Jesus showed his love for God and for us. He told Cornelius about how Jesus died on the cross for all people. Then he told him that Jesus rose from the dead on the third day.

Peter invited Cornelius and his family to believe in Jesus. He said, "All who have faith in Jesus will receive forgiveness of sins." Cornelius and his family felt the Holy Spirit fill them. They believed and had faith. Peter then baptized them all.

BASED ON ACTS OF THE APOSTLES 10:30-48

? Who tells you about Jesus?

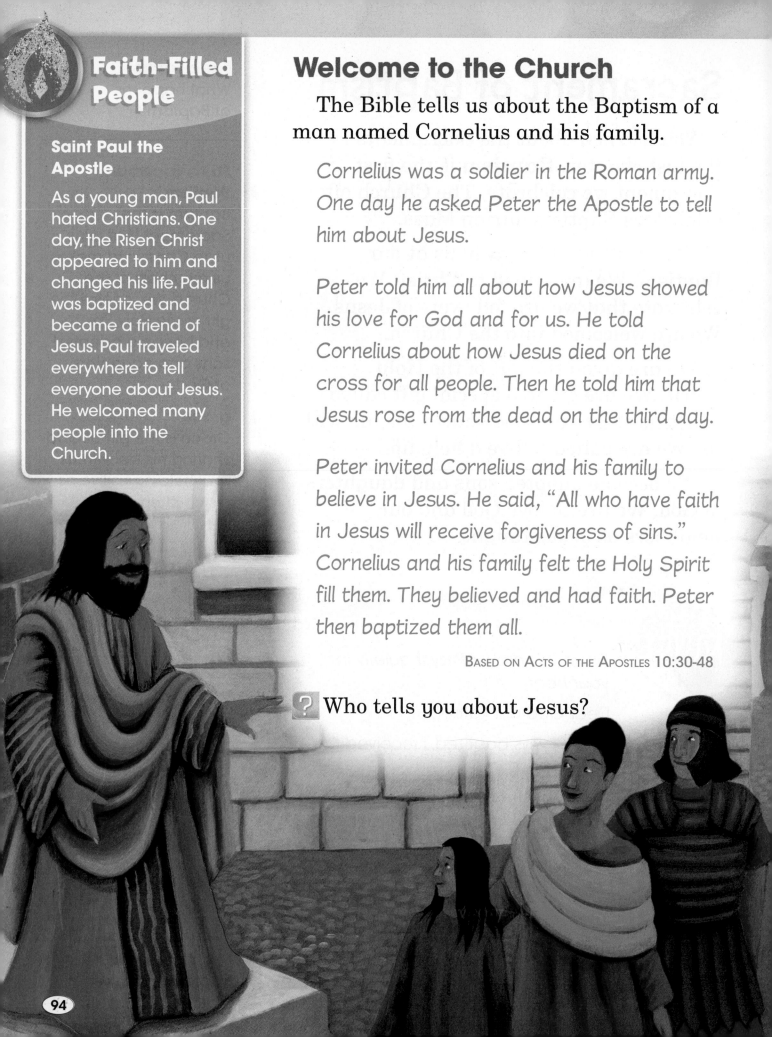

Share in God's Life

We celebrate Baptism with words and actions. We are dipped into the water or water is poured over our head three times. The priest or deacon prays, "I baptize you in the name of the Father, and of the Son, and of the Holy Spirit."

Next, the priest or deacon anoints, or blesses, the top of our head with special oil. We are then dressed in a white garment, and receive a lighted candle.

The words and actions of Baptism show that we share in God's life. They remind us that we are followers of Jesus. We are to live as followers of Jesus, the Light of the world. We are to be lights in the world as Jesus is.

Activity

In each box, draw a picture to help you remember what happens with each object when we celebrate Baptism.

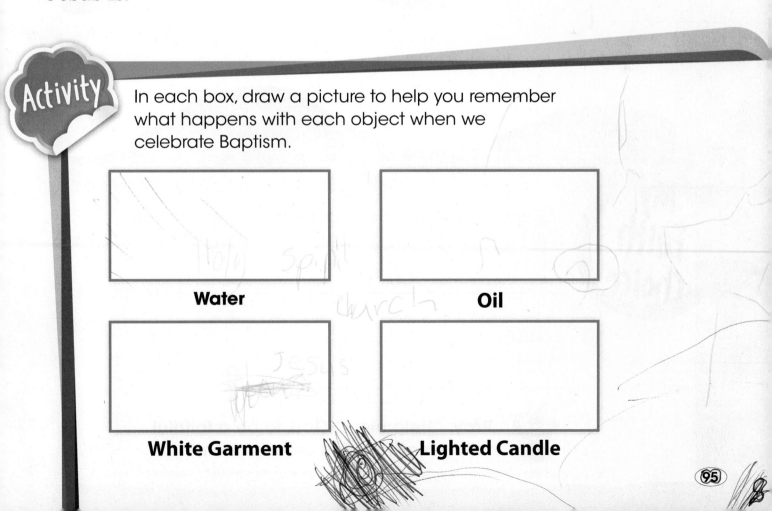

Water

Oil

White Garment

Lighted Candle

I Follow Jesus

Every time you live your faith in Jesus, you show your love for God. The Holy Spirit helps you to live as a faithful follower of Jesus. He helps you to be a light in the world.

Activity

Faithful Ways

Think of how the Holy Spirit helps you live out your Baptism and your faith. On the pathway, write three things you can do to live your faith.

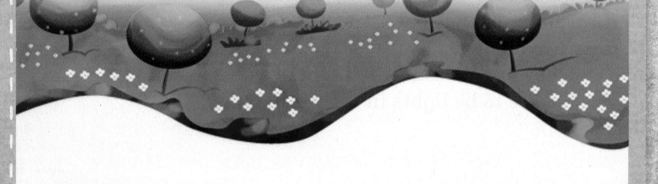

My Faith Choice

This week, I will try to live as a faithful follower of Jesus. I will try my best to be a light in the world. I will

_____

_____

_____.

 Pray, "Help me, O God, to be a faithful follower of your Son Jesus. Amen."

Chapter Review

Find and circle the Sacrament words in the puzzle.
Use the words that you circled in sentences.

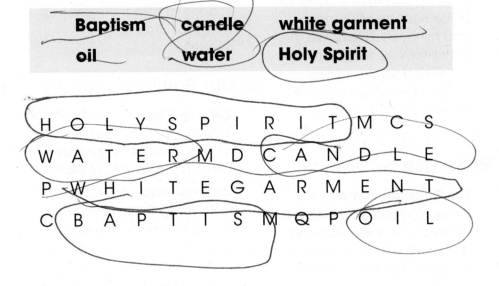

Baptism	candle	white garment
oil	water	Holy Spirit

H O L Y S P I R I T M C S
W A T E R M D C A N D L E
P W H I T E G A R M E N T
C B A P T I S M Q P O I L

TO HELP YOU REMEMBER

1. Baptism is the first Sacrament we receive.

2. The Sacrament of Baptism joins us to Christ and makes us members of the Church.

3. The words and actions of Baptism show that we share in God's life.

Glory to God

A prayer of adoration gives glory to God.

Leader   Let us give glory to God our Father.

All   **Glory to God, now and forever.**

Leader   Let us bless ourselves. (All come forward and bless themselves.)

All   **Glory to God, now and forever. Amen.**

With My Family

This Week . . .

In Chapter 10, "Our Church Welcomes Us," your child learned:

▶ Baptism is the first Sacrament we receive.

▶ Baptism joins us to Christ and makes us members of the Church. We receive the gift of the Holy Spirit. We receive the gift of sanctifying grace. We are made adopted sons and daughters of God.

▶ The Church uses water and oil in the celebration of Baptism.

▶ The virtue of faith is a gift from God that gives us the power to come to know God and believe in him. Living as a faithful follower of Jesus means living out our Baptism.

For more about related teachings of the Church, see the *Catechism of the Catholic Church,* 1213–1284, and the *United States Catholic Catechism for Adults,* pages 183–197.

■ Sharing God's Word

Read together Acts of the Apostles 10:1-49, the account of the Baptism of Cornelius and his family. Emphasize that at Baptism, we receive the gift of the Holy Spirit and become adopted sons and daughters of God.

■ We Live as Disciples

The Christian home and family is a school of discipleship. Choose one of the following activities to do as a family, or design a similar activity of your own:

▶ After Mass this week, visit the baptismal font in your parish church. Talk about why the Church uses water and other baptismal symbols.

▶ Invite all family members to send thank-you notes to their godparents for all they have done to help them grow up in a life of faith.

■ Our Spiritual Journey

Water is a sign of your Baptism, symbolizing dying to sin, rising to new life, and being made a sharer in the very life of God.

How often each day do you drink water? These times are natural moments to reflect on your dignity as a Christian and your spiritual journey. Invite your children to pray each day, "Thank you, God, for the gift of my Baptism."

For more ideas on ways your family can live as disciples of Jesus, visit **www.BeMyDisciples.com**

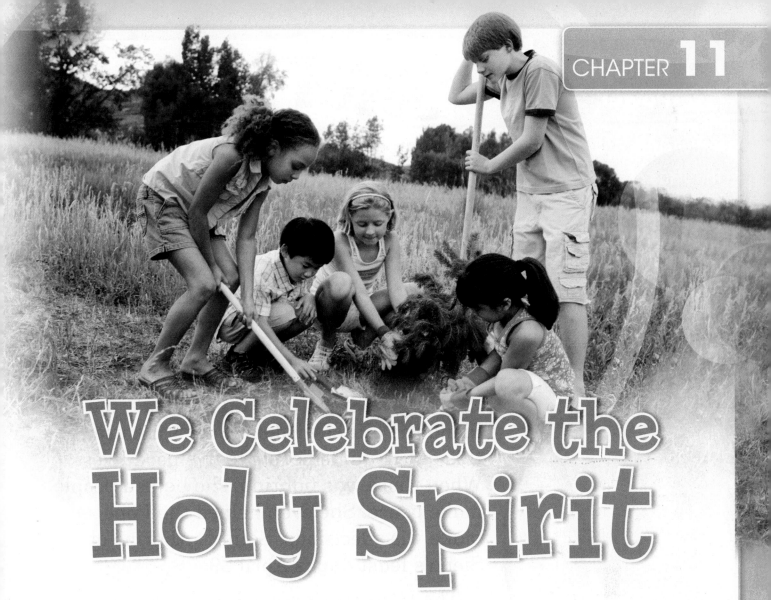

CHAPTER 11

We Celebrate the Holy Spirit

? What special gifts or talents do you have?

Saint Paul reminds us we all have special gifts.

There are different gifts, but one Spirit. The Spirit gives all these gifts so that we can use them to do good things.

BASED ON 1 CORINTHIANS 12:4-11

? How can you use your gifts to help others?

Knowledge

The virtue of knowledge is one of the Gifts of the Holy Spirit. Knowledge helps us better hear and understand the meaning of the Word of God.

The Church Follows **Jesus**

Two Gifted Saints

The Holy Spirit gives us many gifts to share. The Saints of the Church show us many ways to use those gifts. Saint Catherine of Siena and Saint Thomas Aquinas are two of these Saints.

The Holy Spirit gave Saint Catherine of Siena the gift of wisdom. Catherine used this gift to guide people to live good lives. When there was fighting, she helped people make peace. She even helped the Pope make wise decisions. Saint Catherine of Siena's feast day is April 29.

The Holy Spirit gave Saint Thomas Aquinas the gift of knowledge. Thomas wrote many books about the Catholic faith. He helped people learn about their faith. We celebrate his feast on January 28.

 How did these two Saints use their gifts?

Confirmation

We receive the Sacrament of **Confirmation** after Baptism. In Confirmation, we celebrate and receive the gift of the Holy Spirit.

The Holy Spirit is our teacher, helper, and guide. In Baptism, the Holy Spirit gives us seven **spiritual gifts**. These seven special Gifts of the Holy Spirit are wisdom, understanding, right judgment, courage, knowledge, piety, and wonder and awe. These gifts are increased in Confirmation. These gifts help us live our Baptism. They help us better love God and others.

The Holy Spirit guides us in our daily lives. He helps us show our love for God by using our gifts to help others.

Faith Focus
What happens at Confirmation?

Faith Vocabulary
Confirmation
Confirmation is the Sacrament in which the gift of the Holy Spirit strengthens us to live our Baptism.

spiritual gifts
The Holy Spirit gives us spiritual gifts to help us love and serve other people, and so show our love for God.

Activity

Knowledge is one of the Gifts of the Holy Spirit. Draw or write about how you can use this gift.

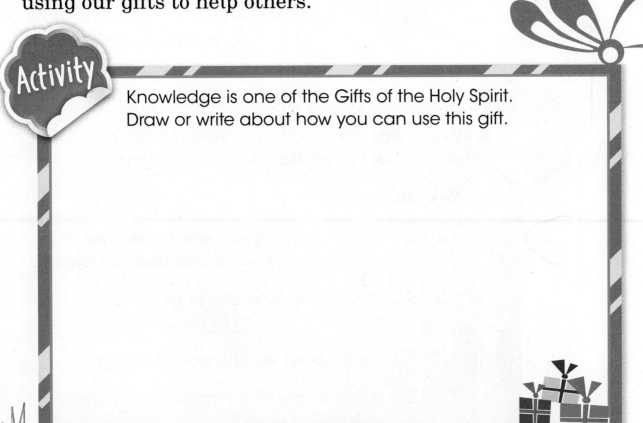

Saint Stephen

Stephen helped the Apostles as a deacon. Stephen used the gift of courage to bravely tell everyone about Jesus. Some people, who were not followers of Christ, did not like what Stephen was doing. They killed him because he was telling everyone about Jesus. The Church celebrates the feast of Saint Stephen on December 26.

Using Our Spiritual Gifts

You have learned that Saint Paul wrote many letters to the first Christians. In these letters, he reminded them to use their gifts. Here is advice he wrote to Christians living in Rome:

> You are all part of the Body of Christ. The Holy Spirit gives you different gifts. You must use your gifts to share God's love with others.
>
> Show that you love one another. Turn away from what is wrong. Be brave. Do what is right and good. Care for one another. Respect one another. Trust in God's promises and be full of hope. Pray and live together in peace.

BASED ON ROMANS 12:5-6, 9-12, 18

Activity

Check **Yes**, if the person is using gifts to share God's love. Check **No**, if the person is not.

Yes   No

☐   ☐   Cameron is a good reader. He does not want to help his little brother learn to read.

☐   ☐   Yelina sings well. She sings with the children's choir at Mass.

☐   ☐   Diego prays with his sick grandfather.

☐   ☐   Linh is funny, so she makes fun of other children at school.

Celebrating Confirmation

In Confirmation, the Holy Spirit strengthens us to live our Baptism. The Holy Spirit helps us to use our gifts and share God's love with others.

We celebrate the Sacrament of Confirmation after we are baptized. If we are baptized as infants, we receive this Sacrament when we are older. Grown-ups who are baptized receive Confirmation right after their Baptism.

The bishop usually leads the celebration of Confirmation. During the celebration, he holds hands in the air and prays, "Send your Holy Spirit upon them to be their Helper and Guide." Next, he prays that we will receive Gifts of the Holy Spirit.

Then the bishop places his right hand on top of our heads. He signs our foreheads with the Sacred Chrism as he prays, "Be sealed with the Gift of the Holy Spirit." We respond, "Amen."

How will you be a follower of Jesus?

Catholics Believe

Sacred Chrism

Sacred Chrism is special oil that the Church uses in the celebration of some of the Sacraments. It is made from olive oil and balsam. At Confirmation, the bishop marks us with Sacred Chrism in the form of the cross. This is a sign we are receiving the gift of the Holy Spirit.

I Follow Jesus

God invites you to open your heart to the Holy Spirit. God wants you to use the spiritual gifts you have been given by the Holy Spirit. Three of these gifts are wisdom, courage, and knowledge.

Activity

A Gift from the Heart

Remember that the Holy Spirit has given you spiritual gifts to share. Draw yourself in the heart shape caring for the needs of others.

My Faith Choice

This week, I will use the gift of

_____.

I will

_____.

Pray, "Thank you, Holy Spirit, for the gifts you have given me. Help me use my gifts to help others. Amen."

Chapter Review

Circle the word that best completes each sentence.

1. The Church needs the _____ of each person.

    books   gifts   pictures

2. The Holy Spirit is our _____, helper, and guide.

    priest   parent   teacher

3. The gift of _____ helps us understand God's Word.

    knowledge   wisdom   wonder

4. In Confirmation, the Church uses _____.

    water   Sacred Chrism   ashes

5. The _____ usually leads the celebration of Confirmation.

    deacon   priest   bishop

▶ TO HELP YOU REMEMBER

1. Confirmation is received after the Sacrament of Baptism.

2. In Confirmation, the Holy Spirit gives us spiritual gifts to help us love and serve God and one another.

3. The Sacrament of Confirmation strengthens us to live our Baptism.

Send Your Spirit

Leader Let us pray that we may always use the Gifts of the Holy Spirit. O God, send your Spirit

All **into our hearts that we may love,**

Leader O God, send your Spirit

All **into our minds that we may understand,**

Leader O God, send your Spirit

All **into our lives that we may serve.**

Leader Holy Spirit, be our teacher and helper.

All **Amen.**

With My Family

This Week . . .

In Chapter 11, "We Celebrate the Holy Spirit," your child learned:

▶ We receive the Sacrament of Confirmation after we receive the Sacrament of Baptism.

▶ The Church uses the actions of the laying on of hands and the anointing with Sacred Chrism in the celebration of Confirmation.

▶ In the Sacrament of Confirmation, we receive and celebrate the Holy Spirit and his seven gifts.

▶ The gift of knowledge is one of the seven Gifts of the Holy Spirit. It enables us to discern the meaning of God's Word.

For more about related teachings of the Church, see the *Catechism of the Catholic Church*, 1285–1314 and 1830–1845, and the *United States Catholic Catechism for Adults*, pages 203–209.

■ Sharing God's Word

Read together 1 Corinthians 14:1, 12. Share the gifts your family has to help others and to build up the Church. Talk about how you use them to be lights in the world.

■ We Live as Disciples

The Christian home and family is a school of discipleship. Choose one of the following activities to do as a family, or design a similar activity of your own:

▶ After Mass this week, visit the place where the sacred oils are kept. Explain that this place is called the ambry. Point out the three containers holding the holy oils; OI stands for Oil of the Sick, OC stands for Oil of Catechumens, and SC stands for Sacred Chrism.

▶ Name some of the times you have seen one another using the gift of courage or knowledge at home. Talk about these as they are moments you are living your Baptism and are "lights" to one another.

■ Our Spiritual Journey

Almsgiving, or sharing our blessings with others, is one of the three major spiritual disciplines of the Church. While we are used to sharing our material blessings, such as money and food, with those in need, we are also to share our spiritual blessings. Encourage your children to give a portion of any money they receive for the good of others and the Church.

For more ideas on ways your family can live as disciples of Jesus, visit **www.BeMyDisciples.com**

CHAPTER 12

We Celebrate Forgiveness

❓ What do you say when you need forgiveness?

Listen carefully to what happens in Heaven when someone asks forgiveness for doing wrong.

There is great joy in heaven for one who asks for forgiveness. BASED ON LUKE 15:7

❓ Why do you think this causes great joy in Heaven?

Disciple Power

Forgiveness

Forgiveness is a sign of love. We ask for forgiveness because we love God. We want everything to be right again. We share God's forgiving love with others when we forgive people who hurt us.

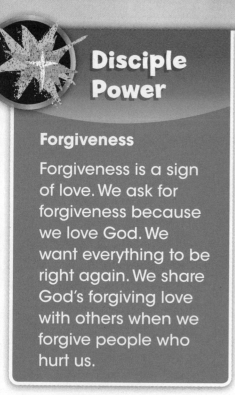

Saint John Vianney

Jesus taught his followers about forgiveness. He taught them that they are to forgive over and over again.

Saint John Vianney was a priest. He was honored and respected because of his kindness to people who were sorry for their sins. Through forgiveness, he showed people God's mercy and love.

There is a story that a special railroad track was built to the village where Father John Vianney lived. The railroad track was built because so many people from all over France wanted to come to John Vianney to confess their sins.

John Vianney was named a Saint in 1925. He is the patron Saint of parish priests.

❓ How was Saint John Vianney a sign of God's forgiving love?

Penance and Reconciliation

Each day we make many choices. Most of the time we make good choices. Sometimes we choose to do or say something that we know God does not want us to do or say. This is called a **sin**. Sometimes we may choose not to do or say something we know God wants us to do. This also is a sin. Sin always harms our friendship with God and with other people.

When we sin, we need to ask for forgiveness. We need to say, "I am sorry. Please forgive me." We also need to make things better when we sin. This shows we are truly sorry for our sins.

God forgives us when we say we are sorry for our sins.

Activity

Practice signing, "I'm sorry."

I'm

sorry.

The Forgiving Father

Jesus told a story about forgiveness.

A father had two sons. The younger son told his father, "I want my share of the family's money now." The father gave the son his share of the family money. The son left home and quickly wasted his money. He thought about his home and his father. He was very sorry for what he had done and decided to return home.

The father saw his son walking toward the family home. The father ran down the road to welcome his son back home. He hugged his son and kissed him. The son said, "Father, I am very sorry."

The father was so happy that he gave a big party to celebrate.

BASED ON LUKE 15:11-24

? What do you think Jesus was teaching about God in this story?

We Celebrate Reconciliation

We too need to ask for forgiveness when we sin. Jesus gave us a Sacrament to help us do this. It is called the Sacrament of **Penance and Reconciliation**.

In this Sacrament, we share in God's mercy and forgiving love. God is always ready to forgive us if we are sorry for our sins. Our sins are forgiven. We receive God's grace. God's grace helps us to make good choices to live as children of God. We receive the gift of peace.

Every celebration of this Sacrament always has four parts. The four parts are:

Catholics Believe

Act of Contrition

When we celebrate the Sacrament of Penance and Reconciliation, we pray an act of contrition. In this prayer, we tell God we are sorry for our sins, we ask for forgiveness, and tell God we will try our best to not sin again.

1. **Confession.** We meet with the priest by ourselves and tell him our sins.

2. **Contrition.** We tell God we are truly sorry for our sins. We pray an act of contrition.

3. **Penance.** We are given a penance. Doing our penance helps repair, or heal, the harm we have caused by our sins.

4. **Absolution.** The priest lays his hands on or over our heads while he says a special prayer. The words and actions of the priest tell us we have received God's forgiveness.

Activity Look at the picture on this page. Under the picture, write the name of the part of the Sacrament of Penance and Reconciliation that is shown.

I Follow Jesus

In the Sacrament of Penance and Reconciliation, God forgives you. You need to forgive others as God forgives you. When you forgive others, you are acting with kindness. You are a peacemaker.

Activity

Sharing God's Gift of Forgiveness

Fill in the empty spaces. Describe how you can be a peacemaker.

I can ask the Holy Spirit to help me live as a peacemaker.

I can forgive _____.

I can show my forgiveness by saying _____.

I can show my forgiveness by doing _____.

My Faith Choice

This week, I will forgive others. I will do what I have written on the lines above.

Pray, "Thank you, Father, for your mercy and kindness. Holy Spirit, teach and help me to be forgiving as Jesus taught. Amen."

Chapter Review

Complete the sentences. Use the words in the word bank.

Absolution	Confession
Contrition	Penance

1. _____ is the telling of our sins to the priest.

2. _____ is true sorrow for our sins.

3. _____ is making up for our sins.

4. _____ is receiving God's forgiveness for our sins.

▶ **TO HELP YOU REMEMBER**

1. Sin is choosing to do or say something against God.

2. In the Sacrament of Penance and Reconciliation, we ask for and receive forgiveness for our sins.

3. Contrition, confession, penance, and absolution are always part of Reconciliation.

Prayer of Petition

In a prayer of petition, we believe and trust that God hears our prayers and will help us.

Leader Let us pray. Lord, our God, you always forgive us because of your great love.

All **Fill our hearts with joy.**

Leader Lord, our God, you always forgive us.

All **Fill our hearts with peace. Amen.**

With My Family

This Week . . .

In Chapter 12, "We Celebrate Forgiveness," your child learned:

▶ Jesus gave the Church the Sacrament of Penance and Reconciliation.

▶ Sin harms our relationship with God and others. When we sin, we need to seek forgiveness.

▶ In the Sacrament of Penance and Reconciliation, we ask for and receive God's forgiveness for the sins we have committed after Baptism. This Sacrament reconciles us with God and with the Church.

▶ When we practice the virtue of forgiveness, we offer God's forgiving love to others.

For more about related teachings of the Church, see the *Catechism of the Catholic Church*, 545–546, 587–590, 976–983, 1420–1484, and 1846–1848, and the United States *Catholic Catechism for Adults*, pages 234–243.

Sharing God's Word

Read together Luke 15:11-24, the parable of the Prodigal Son (Forgiving Father). Or read the adaptation of the parable on page 110. Emphasize the joy of the forgiving father when his prodigal son returned home. Talk about the joy and peace the members of your family experience when you forgive one another.

We Live as Disciples

The Christian home and family is a school of discipleship. Choose one of the following activities to do as a family, or design a similar activity of your own:

▶ Discuss ways your family members ask for forgiveness and forgive one another. Discuss why it is important to forgive one another. Emphasize that when we forgive someone it does not mean that what the person did to hurt us is all right.

▶ Ask each family member to name some of the ways they have been a peacemaker at home. Promise to help one another live as a family of peacemakers. At dinnertime this week, pray to the Holy Spirit to help you live as peacemakers.

Our Spiritual Journey

At the heart of Jesus' work is forgiveness and reconciliation. The Hebrew word *mercy* cannot be easily translated into English. It points to the infinite mercy of God and the undeserved and limitless nature of divine forgiveness. This is the forgiveness we are to show others. Pray the Prayer of Petition for forgiveness with your family this week.

For more ideas on ways your family can live as disciples of Jesus, visit **www.BeMyDisciples.com**

Unit 3 Review

Name _____

A. Choose the Best Word

Complete the sentences. Color the circle next to the best choice for each sentence.

1. The Seven _____ are signs of God's love for us.

○ Bibles   ○ Sacraments   ○ prayers

2. Water and oil are used in the Sacrament of _____.

○ Baptism   ○ Penance and Reconciliation
○ Matrimony

3. Jesus told the story of the Forgiving _____ to teach us about God's forgiveness.

○ Son   ○ Brother   ○ Father

4. In the Sacrament of Confirmation, we receive _____.

○ Jesus   ○ spiritual gifts   ○ forgiveness

5. _____ is freely choosing to do or say something we know God does not want us to do or to say.

○ Penance   ○ Reconciliation   ○ Sin

B. Show What You Know

Draw a line to connect each clue to the correct Sacrament.

Sacrament	Clue
1. Baptism	**a.** strengthens us by the Holy Spirit
2. Confirmation	**b.** forgives sins committed after Baptism
3. Penance and Reconciliation	**c.** first Sacrament we receive

C. Connect with Scripture

What was your favorite story about Jesus in this unit? Draw something that happened in the story. Tell your class about it.

D. Be a Disciple

1. What Saint or holy person did you enjoy hearing about in this unit? Write the name here. Tell your class what this person did to follow Jesus.

_____

2. What can you do to be a good disciple of Jesus?

_____

_____

Part Two

"Thank You, Jesus"

One day, Jesus met ten sick people by the side of the road. They had an awful sickness called leprosy.

When the ten saw Jesus, they called out to him. "Jesus, help us!" they shouted. "Jesus, have mercy on us!" they cried.

Jesus healed all ten people. As they were leaving, one of the ten turned right around to thank Jesus. "Praise God!" he shouted. "Thank you, Jesus!"

Jesus smiled and said, "Go on your way, your faith has made you well."

BASED ON LUKE 17:11-19

What I Have Learned

What is something you already know about these faith concepts?

the Liturgy of the Word

_____

_____

mission

_____

_____

Faith Words to Know

Put an **X** next to the faith words you know.
Put a **?** next to the faith words you need
to learn more about.

Faith Words

_____ Mass

_____ the assembly

_____ Liturgy of the
Eucharist

_____ Eucharist

_____ procession

A Question I Have

What question would you like to ask about
the Mass?

_____

CHAPTER 13

We Gather for Mass

❓ **When do families gather to celebrate?**

God invites us to gather to celebrate. Listen to what God says to his people.

Call my people together. Gather all the people. Gather the old, the young, even the babies. Rejoice and celebrate. Worship the Lord, your God! BASED ON JOEL 2:15-16, 23

❓ **When do Catholics gather to worship God?**

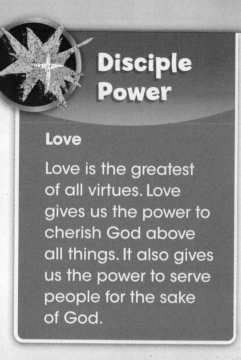

Love

Love is the greatest of all virtues. Love gives us the power to cherish God above all things. It also gives us the power to serve people for the sake of God.

The Church Follows **Jesus**

To Keep the Faith Alive

People in our country are free to worship God. Going to church is not against the law. This was not always true for people in other countries. A long time ago, Christians had to gather in secret to worship God.

Several hundred years ago, the rulers of Ireland made most Catholic priests outlaws. They gathered in secret with other Catholics to celebrate Mass. They celebrated Mass in caves, barns, and other hidden places.

Not long ago, the government of the Czech Republic did not want people to be Catholic. But Father Petr Pit'ha and many other priests continued to gather people for Mass and other Sacraments. All these people had great love for God. Today, Catholics in that country can celebrate their faith without fear.

? Where do you gather to celebrate Mass? Why is it important to go to Mass?

We Gather at Mass

Jesus gathered people on mountainsides, near lakes, and around tables in homes. He gathered people to share the good news of God's love. Jesus promised,

"Where two or three are gathered together in my name, I am there with them."

BASED ON MATTHEW 18:20

After Jesus rose from the dead and returned to God, his disciples came together to pray and listen to God's Word. They remembered Jesus and shared in the Eucharist.

Today we gather too. Every Sunday, we come together to worship God in the celebration of the **Mass**.

At Mass, Catholics gather as an **assembly**. We come to Mass. We pray aloud and sing. We stand and sit and kneel. We show we are disciples of Jesus. Together we worship God the Holy Trinity.

Faith Focus
What happens when we gather for Mass?

Faith Vocabulary

Mass
The Mass is the most important celebration of the Church. At Mass, we gather to worship God. We listen to God's Word. We celebrate and share in the Eucharist.

assembly
The assembly is the People of God gathered to celebrate Mass. All members of the assembly share in the celebration of Mass.

Activity With a partner, talk about all of the things you do at Mass. Choose one thing and act it out for the class.

121

The Mass Begins

The Mass is the most important celebration of the Church. We gather together in church with our Catholic community.

When we gather for Mass, we show that we are disciples of Jesus. We gather to praise God the Father for the great gift of Jesus and for all our blessings.

The Entrance

The Introductory Rites begin the celebration of Mass. The priest or bishop and other ministers enter in procession. Only a priest or bishop can lead us in the celebration of Mass. He wears special clothes called vestments.

We stand and sing. The cantor, or song leader, leads us in the entrance hymn. Singing helps to join us together. We sing our praise and thanks to God.

The Greeting

The priest welcomes or greets us. He leads us in praying the Sign of the Cross. This reminds us how Jesus gave himself for us on the Cross. We also remember our Baptism.

Then the priest greets us with open arms, saying, "The Lord be with you." We respond, "And with your spirit." These words remind us that God is with us in our gathering.

❓ Why do we gather for Mass?

Penitential Act

After the Greeting, the priest invites us to remember God's forgiving love. We pray aloud, asking for the Lord's mercy.

The Gloria

On most Sundays, we sing or pray a special hymn called the "Gloria." It is a beautiful hymn of thanks and praise. This is how it begins.

Glory to God in the highest,

and on earth peace to people of good will.

The Opening Prayer

The priest then says, "Let us pray." We spend a moment in silent prayer. Then the priest leads us in the Opening Prayer. This prayer collects all our prayers and brings them to God the Father in the name of Jesus.

Catholics Believe

The Lord's Day

Sunday is the Lord's Day for Christians. Jesus rose from the dead on Sunday. Catholics remember Jesus by gathering as an assembly on the Lord's Day to celebrate Mass.

A song leader at Mass

Activity

Write the names of those who helped you participate in Mass last Sunday.

- With whom did you assemble?

  _____

- Who led the assembly in song?

  _____

- Who led the assembly in prayer?

  _____

I Follow Jesus

On Sunday, you and your family gather with your Church family to worship God. You offer God thanks and praise together.

Activity

Draw yourself gathered with your Church family for worship. In your picture, show how you are worshiping God at Mass.

The Church Family Gathers

My Faith Choice

I will pay attention at Mass. I will show my love for God by taking part in Mass on Sunday. I will:

_____

_____

Pray, "Gather me in your love, O God, so I can offer you praise. Amen."

Chapter Review

Number the sentences in the order in which they happen at Mass.

_____ **A.** The priest greets us, and we pray the Sign of the Cross.

_____ **B.** We sing or pray aloud the "Gloria."

_____ **C.** The priest leads us in the Opening Prayer.

_____ **D.** We pray for the Lord's mercy.

_____ **E.** The priest enters in procession.

Praise God

At Mass, we offer God thanks and praise. We pray aloud or sing with joy. Pray this psalm with your class.

Leader Loving God, we gather in your name to give you thanks and praise.

Group 1 Shout with joy to God, all the Earth. Worship the Lord with gladness. Come before him singing for joy.

All **Shout with joy to God, all the Earth.**

Group 2 The Lord our God is good;
He is kind and merciful.
His faithful love lasts forever.

All **Shout with joy to God, all the Earth.**

BASED ON PSALM 100

With My Family

This Week . . .

In Chapter 13, "We Gather for Mass," your child learned that:

▶ The Mass is the Church's most important celebration.

▶ At Mass, we gather as an assembly—the Church, the People of God. Together we take part in the Eucharistic celebration.

▶ The celebration of Mass begins with the Introductory Rites. We prepare ourselves for the celebration of God's Word and of the Eucharist.

▶ The virtue of love empowers us to love God and love others because of our love for God.

For more about related teachings of the Church, see the *Catechism of the Catholic Church*, 1322–1332, 1346, 1348, and the *United States Catholic Catechism for Adults*, pages 215–227.

■ Sharing God's Word

Read Acts of the Apostles 2:42-47 together. It is an account of the gathering of the early Church. Emphasize that from the beginning of the Church, Christians gathered to listen to the teachings and writings of the Apostles and to celebrate the Eucharist.

■ We Live as Disciples

The Christian home and family is a school of discipleship. Choose one of the following activities to do as a family, or design a similar activity of your own:

▶ Form the habit of reading the upcoming readings of the week before Mass. You can find them at the *Be My Disciples* Web site or in special books for this purpose. On the way home, discuss the readings and the celebrant's homily.

▶ Talk about the different ways your family gets ready to gather for Mass. Point out that these activities are all part of preparing to celebrate the Eucharist. These moments, too, can be a form of prayer.

■ Our Spiritual Journey

The Theological Virtues of faith, hope, and love invite and empower us to glorify God in all we say and do. Deepen your understanding of these virtues. They are the driving power that enables you to respond and give direction to your response, "Here I am. Lord. Send me." Teach this prayer to your child.

For more ideas on ways your family can live as disciples of Jesus, visit **www.BeMyDisciples.com**

CHAPTER 14

We Listen to God's Word

 What stories or words do you like to hear over and over?

Here is a story we hear at Mass. Jesus was helping people in a village. He was teaching them about God's love. Then something surprising happened.

> A woman said in a loud voice, "Blessed is your mother to have such a wonderful son." Jesus said to the woman, "Blessed are those who hear the Word of God and keep it." BASED ON LUKE 11:27-28

What does it mean to keep the Word of God?

Compassion

Compassion means to care about others when they are hurt or feeling sad. Having compassion makes us want to help them feel better.

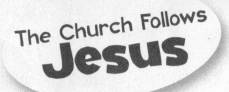

The Church Follows **Jesus**

Announcing God's Word

Jesus told us that he is the Word of God. When we listen to Jesus and do what he says, we are blessed. We are friends of God. But what if you could not hear God's Word?

The Catholic Church helps everyone come to know Jesus. They show compassion to all who need help.

Deaf people can learn to hear and share God's Word. They use a language of hand gestures called American Sign Language, or ASL.

In many parishes, someone uses these hand gestures to sign the words the priest and others say aloud. The deaf people sign their responses.

Activity Learn to sign this word that we say or sing at Mass.

ALLELUIA!

The Liturgy of the Word

Faith Focus
What happens when we celebrate the Liturgy of the Word?

Faith Vocabulary
Liturgy of the Word
The Liturgy of the Word is the first main part of the Mass. God speaks to us through the readings from the Bible.

After the Introductory Rites, we celebrate the **Liturgy of the Word**. The Liturgy of the Word is the first main part of the Mass. We listen and respond to God's Word.

The Readings from the Bible

At Mass on Sundays and on Saturday evenings, we listen to three readings. We sit for the first two readings.

The First Reading is usually from the Old Testament. After this reading, we sing or pray the Responsorial Psalm. Then we hear the Second Reading. It is from the New Testament.

A reading from one of the four Gospels comes next. We get ready to listen to the Gospel by standing and singing or praying aloud the Gospel Acclamation. This is a short hymn of praise. On most days, we stand and sing, "Alleluia."

Why do you think we sing or say, "Alleluia," before we listen to the Gospel?

129

Faith-Filled People

Saint Paul Chong Ha-sang

Catholic lay people, not priests or nuns, first brought the Word of God to the people of Korea. One of those laypeople was Paul Chong Ha-sang. Korea's leaders did not want Christians there. Paul worked all his life to share God's Word. The feast day of Saint Paul Chong Ha-sang is September 20.

We Listen to God's Word

The deacon or priest proclaims the Gospel. The Gospel is the Good News of Jesus Christ. We stand to show our respect.

Listen to this Gospel reading. Jesus said,

"A farmer went out to scatter some seeds. Some seeds fell on a path. Birds ate them up. Some fell on rocks. They dried up and died. Some seeds fell among thorns. The thorns grew and choked the seeds. Other seeds fell on good soil. They took root, grew strong, and produced good fruit.

"The seed is like God's word. People are like the places where the seed fell. . . . Some people do not listen to God's word or they forget it. They are like the rocks and thorns.

But some people really listen to God's word. They respond to it by living good lives. These people are like the good soil. Faith in God grows strong in them."

BASED ON MATTHEW 13:1-9, 18-23

When the Gospel reading is over, we respond, "Praise to you, Lord Jesus Christ."

? How are people who listen to God's Word like the good soil?

We Respond to God's Word

The Homily

After the Gospel is proclaimed, we sit. The priest or deacon talks to us. He helps us to understand the readings. This is called the homily.

The Profession of Faith

After the homily, we stand. Together we respond to God's Word. We pray aloud a profession of our faith, or a creed of the Church. We profess our faith in God the Father, God the Son, and God the Holy Spirit.

The Prayer of the Faithful

The last part of the Liturgy of the Word is the Prayer of the Faithful. We ask God to help the Church and our country. We pray for other people and for ourselves.

Activity

Number the parts of the Liturgy of the Word in the correct order that they happen during Mass. Work with a partner.

_____ Profession of Faith

_____ Prayer of the Faithful

_____ homily

_____ Responsorial Psalm

_____ Old Testament Reading

_____ New Testament Reading

_____ Gospel

I Follow Jesus

At Mass, you are part of the assembly. You take part in the celebration of Mass in many ways. During the Liturgy of the Word, you listen and respond to the Word of God.

Activity

I Listen and Respond

Draw or write about a Bible story you heard at Mass. Write the title of your story on the line. Share what the story tells you about God's love.

_____

My Faith Choice

The next time I take part in Mass, I will

- ☐ say the responses
- ☐ sing the hymns
- ☐ listen carefully to the readings
- ☐ pray the profession of faith
- ☐ _____.

 Pray, "Open my ears to hear your Word, O God. Open my heart to live it every day. Amen."

Chapter Review

Match each word with its correct description.

Words	Descriptions
_____ **1.** readings	**a.** The priest or deacon helps us understand God's Word.
_____ **2.** homily	**b.** We profess our faith in God the Father, God the Son, and God the Holy Spirit.
_____ **3.** creed	**c.** We listen to God's Word.
_____ **4.** Prayer of the Faithful	**d.** We ask God to help us and other people.

▶ TO HELP YOU REMEMBER

1. The Liturgy of the Word is the first main part of the Mass.

2. The Gospel is the main part of the Liturgy of the Word.

3. At Mass, we listen and respond to the Word of God.

Lord, Hear Our Prayer

Leader Let us pray. God our Father, we ask for your help. We pray for the Church, for our country, for our family, and for our friends. We pray for people who are sick. We pray for all people.

All **Lord, hear our prayer.**

Child For _____, we pray to the Lord.

All **Lord, hear our prayer.**

Leader God our Father, send the Holy Spirit upon all who need your help. We ask this in the name of Jesus.

All **Amen.**

This Week . . .

In Chapter 14, "We Listen to God's Word," your child learned:

▶ The Liturgy of the Word is the first main part of the Mass.

▶ The Gospel is the center of the Liturgy of the Word.

▶ During the Liturgy of the Word, we listen to God's Word and make it part of our lives.

▶ We profess our faith and pray for the living and the dead.

▶ The quality of compassion helps us to respond to the needs of others.

For more about related teachings of the Church, see the *Catechism of the Catholic Church,* 1322–1332, 1346, and 1349, and the *United States Catholic Catechism for Adults,* page 218.

◼ Sharing God's Word

Read 2 Timothy 3:16 together. Discuss how Scripture is a source of knowledge for your family. Talk about ways you can make reading the Scripture something your family can do each day.

◼ We Live as Disciples

The Christian home and family is a school of discipleship. Choose one of the following activities to do as a family, or design a similar activity of your own:

▶ Read to your child every day—stories, the Bible, even the daily paper. Listening to a reading is not only pleasing but helps prepare us to listen to the proclamation of God's Word in the liturgy.

▶ Review the responses for the Liturgy of the Word with your child. These can be found on pages 264–265 in your child's book. Knowing the responses helps us better participate in the Mass.

◼ Our Spiritual Journey

At Mass, the Prayer of the Faithful allows us to pray to God for the needs of others. Helping your child to form the habit of praying for the needs of others helps him or her to see the world through a wider perspective and to remember that God brings all blessings. Pray the prayer on page 133 together at home.

For more ideas on ways your family can live as disciples of Jesus, visit **www.BeMyDisciples.com**

CHAPTER 15

We Give Thanks

? What is a gift you have received?

All good things come from God. Think of your many blessings. Join with all God's people and pray,

"I will join with your people, Lord God.
I will thank you in the great assembly."

BASED ON PSALM 35:18

? What do you want to thank God for?

Thankfulness

Thankfulness is a big part of who we are as disciples of Jesus. We have received wonderful blessings and gifts. Jesus calls us to be a thankful people.

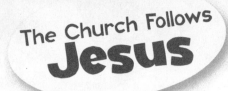

The Church Follows Jesus

Thank You, Lord

Saint Francis of Assisi knew all his blessings came from God. Francis was so full of joy, he often sang his thanks to God.

Catholics thank God for their blessings in many ways. Today the followers of Saint Francis are called Franciscans. The Franciscans in New York City say thanks to God every day. One way they do this is by sharing their blessings with people.

People in New York City who need food or clothing come to the Church of Saint Francis of Assisi. The Franciscans are there every morning to greet them.

The Franciscans give each person sandwiches and something to drink and sometimes clothing to wear. Most importantly, the Franciscans share a smile and words of welcome.

Franciscans continue to share love and respect just as Jesus and Saint Francis did.

? What ways can you and your family share with others as Jesus calls us to do?

The Liturgy of the Eucharist

The Church celebrates the **Liturgy of the Eucharist** as the second main part of the Mass. The word *eucharist* means "thanksgiving." At Mass, we give thanks to God for the gift of Jesus.

The Preparation of the Gifts

The Liturgy of the **Eucharist** begins with the Preparation of the Gifts. Members of the assembly bring our gifts of bread and wine to the altar. The priest tells God all our blessings come from him. We respond, "Blessed be God for ever."

After he washes his hands, the priest invites us to pray. He then leads us in the Prayer over the Offerings. We respond, Amen."

Faith Focus
What happens when the Church celebrates the Liturgy of the Eucharist?

Faith Vocabulary

Liturgy of the Eucharist
The Liturgy of the Eucharist is the second main part of the Mass. The Church does what Jesus did at the Last Supper.

Eucharist
The Eucharist is the Sacrament of the Body and Blood of Jesus Christ.

Activity

Think of the blessings God has given you and your family. Fill the Blessings Bucket with words and images that tell of blessings you have received. Share what is in it with your classmates. Show that you are thankful. Pray with your class, "Blessed be God for ever."

The Eucharistic Prayer

The Eucharistic Prayer is the Church's great prayer of thanksgiving. It is during this prayer that we do what Jesus did at the Last Supper the night before he died.

During the meal, Jesus took bread into his hands and said a blessing prayer. He broke the bread. Giving the bread to his disciples, Jesus said, "Take and eat. This is my body. Do this in memory of me."

Jesus took a cup of wine and gave thanks to God. Giving the cup of wine to his disciples, he said, "Drink it." They all drank from the cup. Jesus said, "This is my blood, which is poured out for many."

BASED ON LUKE 22:17-20

Who says the words of Jesus at Mass?

The Consecration

The priest takes bread and says, "TAKE THIS, ALL OF YOU, AND EAT OF IT, FOR THIS IS MY BODY, WHICH WILL BE GIVEN UP FOR YOU."

Then he takes the cup of wine and says, "TAKE THIS ALL OF YOU, AND DRINK FROM IT, FOR THIS IS THE CHALICE OF MY BLOOD, THE BLOOD OF THE NEW AND ETERNAL COVENANT, WHICH WILL BE POURED OUT FOR YOU AND FOR MANY FOR THE FORGIVENESS OF SINS. DO THIS IN MEMORY OF ME."

These are called the words of Consecration. Through the words of the priest and the power of the Holy Spirit, the bread and wine become the Body and Blood of Christ.

The Communion Rite

After we share a sign of peace, the priest invites us to come forward to receive Holy Communion. We receive the gift of Jesus himself. We receive strength to live as his disciples.

The Communion Rite ends with the Prayer After Communion.

Catholics Believe

The Holy Sacrifice

The Mass is also called the Holy Sacrifice. Jesus' sacrifice on the Cross is the greatest act of love for God the Father and for all people. At Mass, we are made sharers in the sacrifice of Jesus. We join with Jesus and show our love for God. We receive God's grace to love one another as Jesus commanded us to do.

Activity

Complete this sentence:

The bread and wine are changed

to the _____ **and**

_____ **of Jesus Christ.**

I Follow Jesus

At Mass, you receive the gift of the Body and Blood of Christ. One way you can give thanks for the blessings God gives you is by sharing your blessings with other people.

Activity

Sharing My Blessings

Think of how the Holy Spirit helps you share the many blessings you have been given. Write a prayer of thanks to God for all his blessings. Ask the Holy Spirit to help you share your blessings with others.

_____

_____

_____

_____

_____

_____

My Faith Choice

This week, I will share the blessings God has given me. I will

_____

_____.

 Pray, "You have blessed me, O Lord. Teach me and help me to share my blessings. Amen."

Chapter Review

Draw a line from each word in the left column to the sentence it completes in the right column.

Words

Sacrament

Eucharistic Prayer

Last Supper

Sentences

The _____ is the Church's great prayer of thanksgiving.

At the Eucharist, we do what Jesus did at the _____.

The Eucharist is the _____ of the Body and Blood of Christ.

▶ **TO HELP YOU REMEMBER**

1. At the Last Supper, Jesus gave the Church the Sacrament of the Eucharist.

2. At the celebration of the Eucharist, the bread and wine become the Body and Blood of Jesus.

3. We receive the Body and Blood of Jesus in Holy Communion.

Blessed Be God

Blessing prayers tell God we believe that all our blessings come from him. Learn the response, "Blessed be God for ever."

Leader God our Father, we thank you for all your blessings.

All **Blessed be God forever.**

Leader Thank you, God, for _____.

All **Blessed be God forever. Amen.**

With My Family

This Week ...

In Chapter 15, "We Give Thanks," your child learned:

▶ Jesus gave the Church the Sacrament of the Eucharist at the Last Supper.

▶ During the Eucharistic Prayer at Mass, the Church remembers and does what Jesus did at the Last Supper.

▶ At Mass, the bread and wine become the Body and Blood of Jesus through the power of the Holy Spirit and the words of the priest. Jesus is really and truly present under the appearances of bread and wine.

▶ In Holy Communion, we receive the Body and Blood of Jesus.

▶ We thank God for this wonderful gift by the way we live our lives.

For more about related teachings of the Church, see the *Catechism of the Catholic Church*, 1345–1405, and the *United States Catholic Catechism for Adults*, pages 218–220.

■ Sharing God's Word

Read together Luke 22:14-20, part of the account of what happened at the Last Supper. Emphasize that at the Last Supper, Jesus gave the Church the Sacrament of the Eucharist.

■ We Live as Disciples

The Christian home and family is a school of discipleship. Choose one of the following activities to do as a family, or design a similar activity of your own:

▶ This week at Mass, remind your child that what Jesus did at the Last Supper is part of the Eucharistic Prayer. After Mass, talk with your child about the Last Supper and its connection with the Mass. Discuss the importance of receiving Holy Communion.

▶ Sharing family meals together is a practical way to help your child appreciate and understand the meaning of the Eucharist. When your family shares meals together, you are sharing the gift of yourselves. Be sure to give thanks to God by praying Grace Before Meals.

■ Our Spiritual Journey

One of the effects of receiving the gift of the Eucharist in Holy Communion is living out a commitment to the poor. Practicing the spiritual discipline of almsgiving enables us to live out that grace and also to thank God for all his blessings, not only in words but also in our actions.

For more ideas on ways your family can live as disciples of Jesus, visit **www.BeMyDisciples.com**

CHAPTER 16

We Live as Disciples of Jesus

 **When did someone call on you to do something important?**

Each day God calls on us to help him. Close your eyes and imagine you lived many years before Jesus was born. Listen to God calling on you to help him.

The Lord called out, "Who will be my messenger?"

BASED ON ISAIAH 6:8

What message would you share about Jesus with another?

Disciple Power

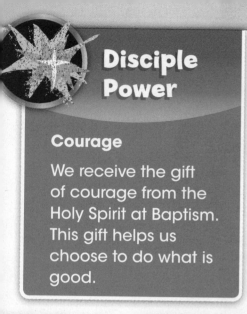

Courage

We receive the gift of courage from the Holy Spirit at Baptism. This gift helps us choose to do what is good.

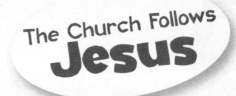

The Church Follows **Jesus**

Spreading the Gospel

God continues to call on people to be missionaries. Missionaries share the message of the Gospel with others. See how these missionaries used courage to listen to God's call.

Jean Donovan

Jean Donovan left her home in Ohio to go to the country of El Salvador. Jean shared God's love and showed her love especially to people who were poor. Jean ran a home for the hungry and the sick. Jean Donovan was killed by people who did not want her to be a missionary in their country.

Saint Frances Cabrini

Frances Cabrini brought her missionary sisters from Italy to New York. They helped the sick and cared for orphans. They built schools and orphanages in the United States and South America. She became so loved by the people they called her "Mother Cabrini."

? If you were a missionary, where would you go? How would you help?

The Concluding Rites

Faith Focus
What does the Mass send us to do?

The Concluding Rites end the celebration of the Mass. We receive God's blessing and go forth to tell others about Jesus.

Final Blessing

The priest asks for God's blessing on us. We bless ourselves with the Sign of the Cross.

Dismissal

The word *mass* means "sending forth." What we have done at Mass, we must now do in the world. We are to be messengers of God by what we say and what we do. That is our work as disciples of Jesus.

The deacon or priest says, "Go in peace, glorifying the Lord by your life." We respond, "Thanks be to God."

Faith Vocabulary
procession
A procession is people prayerfully walking together. It is a prayer in action.

Activity

Draw a picture of yourself sharing one of your gifts or blessings.

Damien was a missionary priest in Hawaii. He went to help the sick people. These people were forced to live and die all alone on an island. Damien helped the sick people take care of one another. He showed them that God loved them very much. Saint Damien's feast day is May 10.

Jesus Gives Us a Mission

At the Last Supper, Jesus told us how we are to glorify God. Listen to what he told his disciples.

At the Last Supper, Jesus tied a towel around his waist and poured water into a bowl. Then he washed his disciples' feet and dried them with the towel.

When he finished, Jesus said, "Here is what you are to do. You are to love one another as I have loved you. Then everyone will know that you are my disciples."

BASED ON JOHN 13:4-5, 13-14, 34-35

Jesus showed his disciples how to glorify God by their lives. We are to love and serve one another. We are to do what he did.

Activity

Discover our mission. Use the code to find out what we must do to love and serve the Lord.

1 = A   2 = E   3 = O

L_V_   _N_   _N_TH_R
   3 2   3 2   1 3   2

_S I H_V_   L_V_D Y_U.
1   1 2   3 2   3

The Concluding Procession

We leave the Church to do what we were sent to do. We leave together in **procession**.

Processions are prayers in action. A procession is people prayerfully walking together. There are five processions at Mass.

1. The entrance procession at the start of Mass

2. The Gospel procession during the Liturgy of the Word

3. The procession of bringing the gifts to the altar at the start of the Liturgy of the Eucharist

4. The procession to receive Holy Communion

5. The procession at the end of Mass

At the end of Mass, we are blessed and sent forth to do the work of Jesus. We are sent from the church to love and serve God and people. We know that the Eucharist gives us the strength to be disciples of Jesus.

? What is the work that Jesus gave us to do?

Catholics Believe

Washing of Feet

Each year on Holy Thursday, the Church celebrates the Evening Mass of the Lord's Supper. At this Mass on Holy Thursday, we celebrate the rite, or ceremony, of the washing of the feet. We remember that we must serve one another as Jesus served us.

I Follow Jesus

You can give glory to God when you live as Jesus taught. You show love to others. You can show courage and do things that are difficult because of your love for God. When you do this, you love God and serve people as Jesus did.

Activity

To Love and Serve

The Holy Spirit helps you to give glory to God. Think of how you will live, love, and serve others with courage. Put a ✔ next to ways you can do this. Act out one of these ways for your class.

_____ I can help out at home.

_____ I can pray for people around the world who suffer from poverty.

_____ I can say no to fighting and arguing with my family.

_____ I can donate some of my toys to children who have less than I do.

_____ I can be a respectful listener at school.

My Faith Choice

I will glorify the Lord this week. I will

_____

_____

_____

Pray, "Help me show my love for you, Lord God, in all I do for others. Amen."

Chapter Review

Number the parts of the Concluding Rites in the correct order.

_____ The Concluding Procession

_____ The Dismissal

_____ The Final Blessing

Bonus Question: What is another word for "sending forth"? _____

Here I Am, Lord

Prayer can help us tell others about God's love. Say this prayer with your class.

Leader	Loving Lord, you ask us to be your messengers.
All	**"Here I am, Lord. Send me."**
Leader	You bless and call us to love one another.
All	**"Here I am, Lord. Send me."**
Leader	You bless us and call us to serve others.
All	**"Here I am, Lord. Send me. Amen."**

With My Family

This Week . . .

In Chapter 16, "We Live as Disciples of Jesus," your child learned:

▶ The Concluding Rites end the celebration of Mass.

▶ In the Concluding Rites of the Mass, we are blessed and sent forth as messengers of the Gospel.

▶ The concluding procession alerts us to the fact that we are sent forth together and are to work together as messengers of the Gospel.

▶ Exercising courage in living as Jesus taught is an important characteristic of Jesus' disciples.

For more about related teachings of the Church, see the *Catechism of the Catholic Church,* 1333–1405 and 1822–1823, and the *United States Catholic Catechism for Adults,* pages 220–227.

■ Sharing God's Word

Read John 13:1-15 and 33-34, the account of Jesus giving the disciples his New Commandment. Or read the adaptation of the story on page 146. Point out how Jesus calls us to serve others as he did. We are to love and serve others as he did.

■ We Live as Disciples

The Christian home and family is a school of discipleship. Choose one of the following activities to do as a family, or design a similar activity of your own:

▶ Review the assembly's responses to the Blessing and Dismissal in the Concluding Rites. Make sure your child knows them by heart. This will help your child participate more fully and actively in the celebration of Mass.

▶ Discuss and decide how your family can glorify God by your lives; for example, by taking part in a service project of your parish that serves your neighborhood or local community.

■ Our Spiritual Journey

Developing the virtues can occur through human effort—diligence, consistent practice, and courage—assisted by God's grace. In this chapter, your child was introduced to the virtue of courage. Model this virtue; help your child learn and practice it through your example.

For more ideas on ways your family can live as disciples of Jesus, visit **www.BeMyDisciples.com**

Unit 4 Review

Name _____

A. Choose the Best Word

Fill in the blanks to complete each of the sentences.
Use the words from the word bank.

> Word   Mass   Amen   Last Supper   assembly

1. The _____ is the most important celebration of the Church.

2. We call the people God gathers to celebrate Mass the _____.

3. The Liturgy of the _____ is the first main part of the Mass.

4. In the Liturgy of the Eucharist, the Church does what Jesus did at the _____.

5. When we receive the consecrated bread and wine in Holy Communion, we say "_____."

B. Show What You Know

Match the items in Column A with those in Column B.

Column A	Column B
1. The Introductory Rites	A. Sacrament of the Body and Blood of Christ
2. knowledge	B. the greatest of all virtues
3. the Eucharist	C. rites that gather and prepare us to worship God
4. the Eucharistic Prayer	D. virtue that helps us to better hear and understand the meaning of God's Word
5. love	E. the Church's great prayer of thanksgiving

C. Connect with Scripture

What was your favorite story about Jesus in this unit? Draw something that happened in the story. Tell your class about it.

D. Be a Disciple

1. *What Saint or holy person did you enjoy hearing about in this unit? Write the name here. Tell your class what this person did to follow Jesus.*

_____

_____

2. *What can you do to be a good disciple of Jesus?*

_____

_____

We Live
Part One

Blessed by God

Jesus was a wonderful teacher. One day Jesus taught his followers eight special ways to live called the Beatitudes. *Beatitude* means "blessing."

Jesus told the crowds that God will bless, or take care of the people who have the most needs. He will also bless those who help others and care for them.

God's Kingdom will belong to those who do what is right.

BASED ON MATTHEW 5:3-10

What I Have Learned

What is something you already know about these faith concepts?

being holy

_____

_____

Ten Commandments

_____

_____

Faith Words to Know

Put an **X** next to the faith words you know.
Put a **?** next to the faith words you need
to learn more about.

Faith Words

____ grace

____ honor

____ rabbi

____ Great
Commandment

____ false witness

____ justice

A Question I Have

What question would you like to ask about living the Ten Commandments?

_____

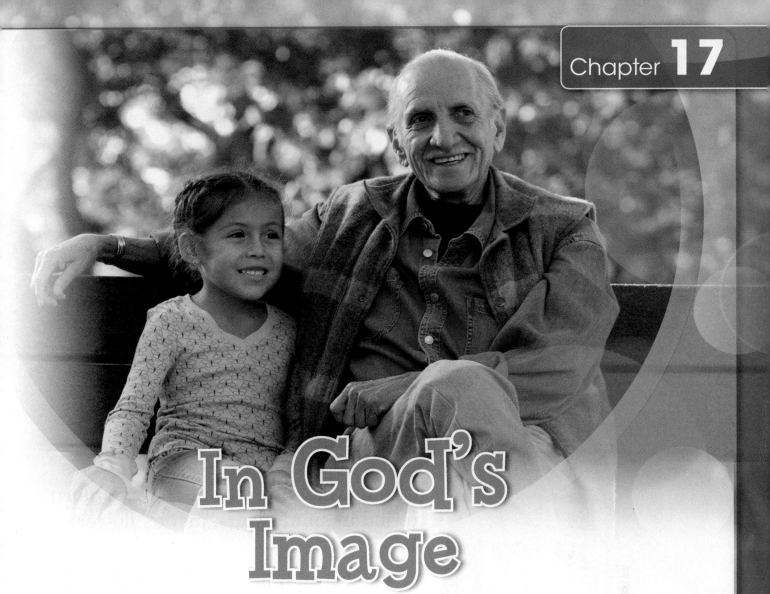

Chapter 17

In God's Image

? Who are some of the people who love you? What are some of the ways they show you they love you?

Listen to find out how much God loves you:

See how very much God the Father loves us. He calls us his own children!

BASED ON 1 JOHN 3:1

? What do you think it means that God calls you his child?

Kindness

We are kind when we do things that show we care. We are kind when we treat other people as we want to be treated.

The Church Follows Jesus

The Little Flower

Thérèse of the Child Jeus was proud to be a child of God. Thérèse tried her best to do little things well.

When she was a young girl, she grew flowers and took care of her pet birds. She treated everyone with kindness.

When Thérèse was fifteen, she became a religious sister. She called herself God's "little flower." She wanted to give glory to God in small ways, just as flowers do.

The Church has named Thérèse a Saint. Her feast day is October 1.

? What are some of the little things that you do to show respect for God and others?

We Are Holy

The Bible teaches that God gives every person a great **honor**. He creates every person in his image and likeness. God shares his life with us. He creates us to be holy. We are children of God.

Jesus taught us to honor God, ourselves, and other people. He taught us to treat people with kindness, respect, and love. Jesus taught us to honor all people as children of God. He said,

"Love God as this child loves him. If you do, God will welcome you into heaven."

Based on Matthew 18:3

Faith Focus
What do we do to live as children of God?

Faith Vocabulary
honor
To honor someone is to treat them with kindness, respect, and love.

Activity

Imagine that you are one of the children in the picture. Act out the scene with a partner. What would you say to Jesus?

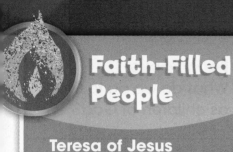
Teresa of Jesus

Saint Teresa of Jesus lived in Spain. The Church honors her as one of the Doctors of the Church. This means that the Church honors her as a great teacher of the faith. The Church celebrates Saint Teresa of Jesus' feast day on October 15.

Jesus Is Our Teacher

The disciples of Jesus honored him in many ways. They called him "Teacher" as a sign of great honor and respect.

Jesus told his disciples:

> *"I am the way, the truth, and the life. I will lead you to God."*
>
> BASED ON JOHN 14:6

Jesus' disciples listened to him carefully and did as he said.

Jesus is our Teacher too. We listen to him. We learn from him. We try our best to live as he taught.

Activity

Follow each path to Jesus. Ask Jesus to teach you to live as a child of God.

Making Good Choices

Jesus taught us how to make good choices. We show that we are proud to be children of God when we make good choices.

We live as children of God when we make good choices. We show that we are trying our best to live as children of God. We grow in kindness. We love God, ourselves, and other people as Jesus did.

God the Holy Spirit helps us to make good choices. He gives us his grace, or help, to make good choices. When we make good choices, we grow as children of God.

❓ Who has helped you make good choices to live as a child of God? How have you helped others? Tell a partner.

I Follow Jesus

The Holy Spirit helps you to make good choices. He helps you to be kind. He helps you be fair. When you are kind and fair, you show that you are proud to be a child of God.

Activity

Living as a Child of God

Write some words of kindness that you say. Then write acts of kindness that you do to show that you are a child of God.

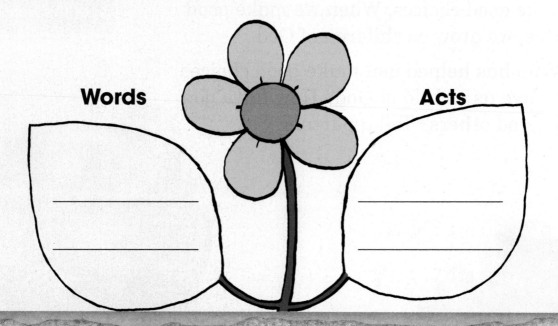

Words

Acts

_____

_____

My Faith Choice

This week, I will surprise someone with this act of kindness. I will

_____

_____

 Pray, "Father, thank you for loving me so much. Help me with your grace to make good choices. Help me to grow as your child. Amen."

Chapter Review

Find and circle the words hidden in the puzzle. Use these words to share with a partner how you can live as a child of God.

respect	kindness	good	love
follow	choices	honor	faith

R E S P E C T L K I N D N E S S

O F O L L O W P N Z T F A I T H

C H O I C E S T R W L O V E P T

Y H O N O R L I G O O D R W Z A

► **TO HELP YOU REMEMBER**

1. All people are to be honored and respected. God has created everyone to be a child of God.

2. Jesus taught that we are to live as children of God.

3. The Holy Spirit helps us to make choices to live as children of God.

May God Bless Us

Pray this prayer to ask God to bless your class. Ask him to help you live as children of God.

Leader   Father, we ask your blessing on us.

All   **Father, we are your children.**

Leader   Guide us to choose what is good and to do your will.

All   **Father, we are your children.**
(Each child comes forward for a blessing.)

Leader   May God bless you and keep you.

All   **Amen.**

With My Family

This Week . . .

In Chapter 17, "In God's Image," your child learned:

▶ We are to honor and respect all people. Every person has the dignity of being a child of God because we are created in the image and likeness of God.

▶ Jesus is our Teacher. He showed us how to live as children of God. He said, "I am the way, the truth, and the life. I will lead you to God" (Based on John 14:6).

▶ We honor and respect Jesus as our Teacher when we try our best to live as he taught.

▶ We grow in the virtue of kindness when we try to have all our words and actions show respect for God, for other people, and for ourselves.

For more about related teachings of the Church, see the *Catechism of the Catholic Church*, 1699–1756 and 1996–2016, and the *United States Catholic Catechism for Adults*, pages 307–309, 324–331, 351–354.

◼ Sharing God's Word

Read Mark 10:13-16 together, "Jesus and the Children." Emphasize that Jesus taught us to love God as children do and to respect all people as children of God.

◼ We Live as Disciples

The Christian home and family form a school of discipleship. Choose one of the following activities to do as a family, or design a similar activity of your own:

▶ Notice when your child makes good choices. Compliment him or her and point out how the Church helps us make good choices. Praise your child for doing his or her best to live as Jesus taught.

▶ Saint Thérèse of Lisieux focused on doing the little things in life out of love. Decide together how your family can live this week as Saint Thérèse did and do the kind things, that are part of daily life, out of love.

◼ Our Spiritual Journey

The *Story of a Soul*, the autobiography of Saint Thérèse of Lisieux, reveals to us the depth of her spirituality. Her childlike simplicity is appealing to young children. Pray these words from a poem of Saint Thérèse together this week: "Come reign within my heart, smile tenderly on me, today, dear Lord, today."

For more ideas on ways your family can live as disciples of Jesus, visit **www.BeMyDisciples.com**

Chapter 18

We Live as Children of God

? What is something you have learned from a catechist?

Here is a prayer from the Bible. Listen carefully to what the person is asking God:

Lord God, help me know and understand your ways; teach me to live the way you want me to live. Help me know and live your truth and teach it to me, for you are my God. BASED ON PSALM 25:4-5

? What would you like to ask God to teach you?

Disciple Power

Fortitude

Fortitude is another word for courage. Fortitude helps us to stay strong, to do our best, and to do what is right and good when it is hard to do so. The Holy Spirit gives us the gift of fortitude to live the way that God wants us to live.

Saint Pedro

Pedro Calungsod lived on the island of Cebu in the Philippines. When he was a teenager, he played sports. He had a job as a carpenter. Pedro became a catechist. He taught others about God and his Son, Jesus.

Pedro left his home to become a missionary to people who did not know about God. Pedro needed courage to do this work. He had to cross over high mountains. He had to go through deep jungles. It was not easy, but Pedro did not give up. He wanted to do his best to teach people about the Holy Trinity.

The people of the Philippines honor Saint Pedro each year with a festival. The Church celebrates his feast day on April 2.

? How did Saint Pedro live the virtue of fortitude, or courage?

A Different Teacher

There were many teachers of God's law during Jesus' time. They were called rabbis. *Rabbi* means "teacher."

Crowds of people followed Jesus everywhere. People wanted to learn about God from him. They said that they had never before heard a teacher like Jesus.

Jesus was different from the other rabbis. All of the religious teachers of Jesus' time relied on other teachers. They needed other respected teachers to prove that their teaching was right, but Jesus did not.

Jesus taught about God on his own. He is God, the Second Person of the Holy Trinity. Jesus said,

"Whoever has seen me has seen the Father." JOHN 14:9.

Faith Focus
What does the Great Commandment help us to do?

Faith Vocabulary
rabbi
Rabbi is a Hebrew word that means "teacher."

Great Commandment
The Great Commandment is to love God above all else and to love others as we love ourselves.

Activity

Find out what Jesus said about himself. Unscramble the sentence.

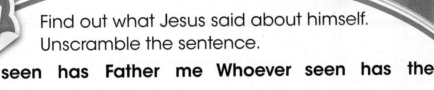

seen has Father me Whoever seen has the

_____ _____ _____

_____ _____ _____

_____ _____ .

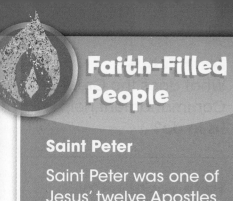

Saint Peter

Saint Peter was one of Jesus' twelve Apostles. He was the first one to recognize that Jesus is the Savior. After he rose from the dead, Jesus asked Peter to care for the Church and all its members. Peter was the first Pope. His feast day is June 29.

Jesus Teaches

One day, a teacher of the Law came to Jesus and asked,

"Rabbi, which commandment of God is the greatest?" Jesus said, "You shall love the Lord your God with all your heart, with all your soul, and with all your mind. This is the first and greatest commandment. The second commandment is like the first one. You shall love your neighbor as yourself."

BASED ON MATTHEW 22:37-40

Together both commandments make up one **Great Commandment**.

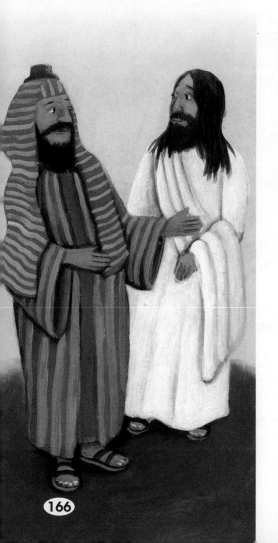

Activity

Read the Scripture verses again. Name the two parts of the Great Commandment.

_____

_____

_____

_____

_____

_____

The Great Commandment

The Great Commandment sums up all of God's laws. The first part of the Great Commandment teaches that God is the center of our lives. Jesus teaches us to love God above all else.

We live the first part of the Great Commandment in many ways. We show our love for God when we honor and respect God in all we do and say. We show our love for God when we pray.

The second part of the Great Commandment teaches us to treat others as we like to be treated. We live this part of the Great Commandment in many ways. We are to respect and honor all people as we do ourselves. We respect and honor others when we help them care for their things. We respect and honor people when we treat them fairly.

? How are the people in the pictures showing love for God and for one another?

I Follow Jesus

Because God loves you, you can love others. The Holy Spirit helps you to live the Great Commandment. You can love God above all else. You can love others as you love yourself.

Activity

Teaching Others

Pretend that you are teaching a class about the Great Commandment. Draw two pictures to show what it means.

Love God	Love Others

My Faith Choice

I will show fortitude and live the Great Commandment this week. I will

_____

_____.

Pray, "Loving God, always be my teacher. Teach me the way to love you and others with all my heart, soul, and mind. Amen."

Chapter Review

Fill in the blank for each sentence.

Great Commandment	fairly	respect

1. The _____ sums up all God's laws.

2. We show we honor God when we _____ his laws.

3. The Great Commandment tells us to treat others _____.

TO HELP YOU REMEMBER

1. Jesus taught that the Great Commandment is the greatest commandment.

2. The first part of the Great Commandment tells us to love God.

3. The second part of the Great Commandment tells us to love other people as we love ourselves.

An Act of Love

God is with us all day long. Take time each day to tell God you love him.

Leader   Let us tell God that we want to live the Great Commandment.

All   **O my God,
I love you above all things.
I love you with my whole heart and soul.
I love my neighbor as myself because of my love for you.
Amen.**

With My Family

This Week ...

In Chapter 18, "We Live as Children of God," your child learned:

▶ Jesus taught that the heart of God's Law is the Great Commandment.

▶ The driving spirit of all God's laws is summarized in two commandments, namely, to love God and love others as yourself.

▶ The gift of fortitude or courage helps us live the Great Commandment.

For more about related teachings of the Church, see the *Catechism of the Catholic Church*, 2052–2055, 2083, and 2196, and the *United States Catholic Catechism for Adults*, pages 307–309.

■ Sharing God's Word

Read Matthew 22:34-40, Jesus' teaching on the Great Commandment, or read the adaptation of the story on page 166. Emphasize that the Great Commandment has two connected parts: love God, and love your neighbor as yourself. This commandment sums up the heart and purpose of God's laws.

■ We Live as Disciples

The Christian home and family form a school of discipleship. Choose one of the following activities to do as a family, or design a similar activity of your own:

▶ Create a large heart out of poster paper. Write the Great Commandment within the heart. Display the heart as a reminder to the whole family to live the Great Commandment.

▶ The Great Commandment tells us to treat others as we would like to be treated. Talk about some of the practical ways that your family is living this part of the Great Commandment. Encourage your children to ask themselves at bedtime how well they lived the Great Commandment that day.

■ Our Spiritual Journey

The moral virtues give us strength to live the moral life, but these virtues are acquired through deliberate effort and much practice. The virtue of fortitude helps us keep the Great Commandment—no simple task. Following the Great Commandment means embracing the Teacher, Jesus himself—or, to be exact, allowing him to embrace us. Help your child memorize the Act of Love on page 169 and pray it together.

For more ideas on ways your family can live as disciples of Jesus, visit **www.BeMyDisciples.com**

Chapter 19

POOL RULES

NO Diving

We Love God

? What is one rule your family has that everyone has to follow?

In the Bible, God tells why he gives us rules. Listen to what the writer of this psalm discovered.

Happy are those who obey God's rules.
Happy are those who keep God's laws. They
are on their way to God. BASED ON PSALM 119:1-3

? Why does obeying God's rules make a person happy?

Disciple Power

Obedience

Authority is a gift from God. God gives people authority to help us follow God's laws. People in authority, such as parents and grandparents, teachers and principals, priests and bishops, deserve respect. The virtue of obedience gives us strength to honor and respect people in authority.

Saint Benedict

Many years ago, a boy named Benedict learned the importance of good rules. At school, he saw that not obeying rules made people very unhappy.

When Benedict was older, he went to the countryside to live on his own. He spent each day praying and reading God's Word. Many families sent their sons to Benedict. They wanted him to teach their children about prayer and the Bible.

Benedict decided to build a monastery where men could live, work, and pray together. His monastery became a place where everyone obeyed the same rules.

Benedict's rules helped the men and others learn how to pray, to love God's Word, and to work together. These rules continue to help many people live holy and happy lives today.

? Which rules would help people in your family live happy and holy lives?

God's Rules

Long ago, God chose Moses to lead his people out of slavery in Egypt. God's people were not living as God wanted them to live. So, God gave Moses the **Ten Commandments**.

The Ten Commandments are God's rules to help all people live happy and holy lives. The Ten Commandments are God's Laws for all people. The first three of the Ten Commandments teach us ways we are to love and honor God. The next seven show us the ways to love and honor all people. All the Commandments teach us how to live as children of God.

Faith Focus
How do the First, Second, and Third Commandments help people to love and respect God?

Faith Vocabulary
Ten Commandments
The Ten Commandments are the laws that God gave Moses. They teach us to live as God's people. They help us live happy and holy lives.

Activity

Write one way you show your love and honor for God.

_____

_____

Write one way you show your love and honor for people.

_____

_____

Faith-Filled People

Saint Scholastica

Scholastica was Saint Benedict's twin sister. She established a monastery for women. She and the nuns living in the monastery followed the rules of Saint Benedict. She is the patron Saint of all nuns. The Church celebrates Saint Scholastica's feast day on February 10.

Keeping God First

The first three Commandments name ways that we are to honor and love God.

1. **I am the Lord your God: you shall not have strange gods before me.**

The First Commandment tells us that there is only one God. We are to worship God alone. We are to have faith in God, to hope in him, and to love him more than all else.

2. **You shall not take the name of the Lord your God in vain.**

The Second Commandment teaches us that God's name is holy. We are always to speak it with respect and love. We are also to show respect for holy people, places, and things.

3. **Remember to keep holy the Lord's Day.**

The Third Commandment teaches us that we are to keep Sunday as the Lord's Day. Each Sunday, Catholics have the responsibility to gather to celebrate the Eucharist.

? What are some ways you can obey the first three Commandments?

Wise Sayings to Live By

The writers of the Bible collected many wise sayings to help us follow God's Law. These wise sayings are called proverbs. You can read them in the Book of Proverbs found in the Old Testament.

This proverb helps us show our love for God.

Trust God with all your heart. Do not think you always have the answers. God will show you the right way.

BASED ON PROVERBS 3:5-6

Catholics Believe

The Bishop's Motto

A motto is a short saying. For example, the motto of the Benedictines is "Work and Pray." Cardinal Donald Wuerl, Archbishop of Washington, DC, uses a motto to describe his work. He chose as his motto "Thy Kingdom Come."

Activity

Use the words in the word bank to find actions that show how to follow the first three of the Ten Commandments. Find and circle each action in the puzzle.

BELIEVE	OBEY	PRAY
REST	WORSHIP	HONOR

```
X  H  P  D  T  Y  G  T  U  O
W  O  R  S  H  I  P  M  J  U
L  N  E  L  H  O  N  O  R  T
D  O  S  L  I  E  B  A  Y  G
V  R  T  B  E  L  I  E  V  E
E  D  S  H  W  P  R  A  Y  D
```

I Follow Jesus

The Holy Spirit always will help you make wise choices. He will give you the grace to obey the Ten Commandments. He will help you make choices to live a happy and holy life.

Activity

Advice for My Family

What good advice can you give your family to help all of you love and honor God? Write your advice here and share it with them.

_____

_____

_____

_____

_____

My Faith Choice

This week, I will show my love for God by

_____

_____

Pray, "Loving God, I am happy to obey your Commandments. Help me grow in love for you more and more each day. Amen."

Chapter Review

Draw lines from the left column to the right column to make correct sentences.

1. God

2. St. Benedict

3. Moses

a. is the one we honor above all others.

b. received the Ten Commandments from God.

c. built a monastery.

Come, Holy Spirit

The Holy Spirit helps you keep God's Commandments. Learn to sign the prayer "Come, Holy Spirit."

Come

Holy Spirit

With My Family

This Week . . .

In Chapter 19, "We Love God," your child learned:

▶ The Ten Commandments guide us in living happy and holy lives.

▶ The first three of the Ten Commandments name ways that we are to love and honor God.

▶ Proverbs in the Bible are short wise sayings that help us to follow God's Law and to live happy and holy lives.

▶ The virtue of obedience strengthens us to show honor to those who have authority. Authority is a gift from God that he gives people to help them live his Law.

For more about related teachings of the Church, see the *Catechism of the Catholic Church*, 2083–2136, 2142–2165, 2168–2188 and 2194, and the *United States Catholic Catechism for Adults*, pages 341–369.

■ Sharing God's Word

Read Exodus 20:1-3, 7-17 together. Emphasize that the Ten Commandments are God's Laws. Talk about how the Ten Commandments help us to live holy and happy lives.

■ We Live as Disciples

The Christian home and family is a school of discipleship. Grow in your love of God together. Choose one of the following activities to do as a family, or design a similar activity of your own:

▶ Make prayer rocks to carry in your pockets. Use them as reminders to set aside time to pray often throughout the day. When you put your hand into your pocket, you will be reminded to pray. You will also be reminded that God is always with you.

▶ Point out and compliment your child when he or she is obedient. Share ways that you, too, are obedient to others. Help your child see that being obedient is showing respect for those in proper authority.

■ Our Spiritual Journey

Remember the Gospel story of Martha and Mary (Luke 10:38-42). It is a story of balancing work and prayer in our daily lives. It is a story about going about our daily lives keeping God at the center of our lives, just as St. Benedict taught in his Rule. Pray together, "Come, Holy Spirit, fill our hearts with your love."

For more ideas on ways your family can live as disciples of Jesus, visit **www.BeMyDisciples.com**

Chapter 20

We Love Others

[?] How do you like other people to treat you?

Listen to what Jesus says about how we are to treat others.

Jesus told his disciples, "Treat other people the same way you want them to treat you." BASED ON MATTHEW 7:12

This is called the Golden Rule.

[?] Why is this a good rule?

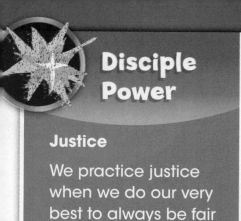

Justice

We practice justice when we do our very best to always be fair to others.

The Church Follows Jesus

Caring for Others

Vincent de Paul lived the Golden Rule. He took care of people who were sick. He gave clothes and food to people who had no money. Vincent treated others as he wanted to be treated. He is a Saint of the Church.

Today, people in Catholic parishes live the Golden Rule as Vincent de Paul did. They are members of the St. Vincent de Paul Society. They live the virtues of charity and justice. They help build a kind and fair world.

? How does your parish live the Golden Rule?

Living the Golden Rule

The Fourth through Tenth Commandments helps us to live the Golden Rule.

4. Honor your father and your mother.

The Fourth Commandment teaches us to honor and obey our parents. We also honor and obey other people whom parents ask to help guide their children.

5. You shall not kill.

The Fifth Commandment teaches us that we are to take care of our own lives and the lives of other people.

6. You shall not commit adultery.

9. You shall not covet your neighbor's wife.

These two commandments teach us that we are to respect our own bodies and the bodies of others. We are not to let people touch us in the wrong way. We are to help families live happy and holy lives.

Faith Vocabulary
covet
We covet when we have an unhealthy desire for something.

false witness
Giving false witness means telling lies.

Activity

Look at the pictures on this page. Describe how the people are showing love for others. With a partner, act out a way you can show love for others too.

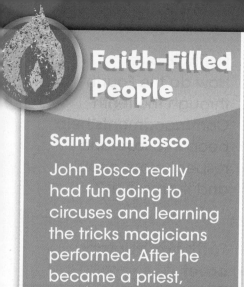

Saint John Bosco

John Bosco really had fun going to circuses and learning the tricks magicians performed. After he became a priest, Father John Bosco gathered children around him and did the tricks for them. As they gathered, Father Bosco taught the children about Jesus. The Church celebrates the feast day of Saint John Bosco on January 31.

7. You shall not steal.

The Seventh Commandment teaches us to respect the property of other people. We are not to steal or cheat.

8. You shall not bear false witness against your neighbor.

The Eighth Commandment teaches that we are to be honest and truthful. We are not to lie. To **bear false witness** means to lie.

10. You shall not covet your neighbor's goods.

Even more than that, the Tenth Commandment tells us not to be jealous of other people or their things. We are also to use food, water, and other things of creation fairly. We are to share our blessings as gifts from God.

When we live all these Commandments, we are living holy lives. When we live the Ten Commandments, we are living as children of God.

? How do the Seventh, Eighth, and Tenth Commandments help you live the Golden Rule?

Share with the Poor

In this story, Jesus teaches us to do more than just obey the Ten Commandments.

One day a man came to Jesus and asked, "Teacher, what must I do to get to heaven?"

Jesus said to the man, "You shall obey the Ten Commandments."

The man told Jesus, "I have always followed all these rules."

Looking at the man Jesus said to him, "There is one more thing you need to do. Give what you have to the poor. Then, come, follow me."

But the man could not do it. He went away sad.

BASED ON MARK 10:17-22

Catholics Believe

Almsgiving

Jesus teaches that we are to do more than obey the Ten Commandments. We are to share what we have with the poor. Almsgiving is one way we do this. *Almsgiving* is a word that means "sharing something to help the poor." The first Christians did this very well. Their neighbors used to say, "See how much they love one another."

Activity

Work with a partner. Write a saying that reminds others to share what they have with people who are poor.

_____

_____

CLOTHING

I Follow Jesus

When you live the Ten Commandments, you are living as a child of God. You are building a kind and fair world. When you keep the Golden Rule and share with the poor, you are doing even more. You are living as a disciple of Jesus.

Activity

Living as a Child of God

The three sentences in the frames name ways to live the Ten Commandments. Choose one. Write or draw how you can do what it says.

> **Respect your parents.**

> **Eat healthful foods.**

> **Tell the truth.**

My Faith Choice

I will keep the Commandments this week. I will do more, as Jesus asked. I will

_____

_____

Pray, "Holy Spirit, teach me and help me to keep the Commandments. I want to honor you, be fair to others, and do even more. Amen."

Chapter Review

Circle Yes if a sentence is true. Circle No if a sentence is not true.

1. The Fourth through the Tenth Commandments show us how to honor, respect, and love God.

   Yes   No

2. The Fourth through the Tenth Commandments show us how to follow the Golden Rule and build a kind and fair world.

   Yes   No

3. Jesus' followers should do more than just obey the Ten Commandments.

   Yes   No

Trust in the Lord!

At Baptism, we receive the grace to live God's Commandments. Pray this prayer. Tell God you will try your best to live as a follower of his Son, Jesus Christ.

Leader   Remember the Lord's teachings. Keep his laws with all your heart.

All   **Lord, teach us your laws.**

Leader   Trust in the Lord with all your heart. The Lord will lead you on a straight path.

All   **Lord, we will always trust in you.**

With My Family

This Week . . .

In Chapter 20, "We Love Others," your child learned:

▶ The Fourth through the Tenth Commandments name ways that we are to love, honor, and respect other people, ourselves, and all of God's creation.

▶ The Golden Rule summarizes the Fourth through the Tenth Commandments.

▶ Jesus taught that we are to do more than just obey the Ten Commandments. We are to share our blessings with the poor.

▶ The Ten Commandments help us live as children of God. They guide us to build a kind and fair world. They help us prepare for the coming of the Kingdom of God.

▶ People who live the virtue of justice work to build a kind and fair world.

For more about related teachings of the Church, see the *Catechism of the Catholic Church*, 2196–2246, 2258–2317, 2331–2391, 2401–2449, 2464–2503, 2514–2527, and 2534–2550, and the *United States Catholic Catechism for Adults*, pages 375–455.

◼ Sharing God's Word

Read Mark 10:17-22, Jesus' teaching on doing more than just obeying the Ten Commandments. As a family, discuss what more your family can do to act as Jesus' disciples and follow him. Name ways your family can be less attached to material possessions.

◼ We Live as Disciples

The Christian home and family is a school of discipleship. Grow in your love for all people as Jesus commanded. Choose one of the following activities to do as a family, or design a similar activity of your own:

▶ Help your children write and illustrate a storybook about how your family shows respect for other people and thus honors God.

▶ Talk about what your parish does to build a just and kind world. Choose a way to support one of these activities.

◼ Our Spiritual Journey

Every person has a call to holiness. Every person has the inner longing to be the person who they were created to be— the image and likeness of God. Living the Ten Commandments is the minimum we can do to travel the road to happiness and holiness. This week at mealtime, pray the prayer on page 185 at the end of the meal.

For more ideas on ways your family can live as disciples of Jesus, visit **www.BeMyDisciples.com**

Unit 5 Review

Name _____

A. Choose the Best Word

Fill in the blanks to complete each of the sentences.
Use the words from the word bank.

almsgiving	honor	Golden Rule
Ten Commandments	grace	Great Commandment

1. The _____ is to love God above all else and to love people as we love ourselves.

2. _____ means sharing something to give to the poor.

3. The _____ are the laws God gave us to help us live happy and holy lives.

4. To _____ a person is to show that person great respect.

5. When we treat others the same way we want them to treat us, we are following the _____.

6. _____ is the gift of God sharing his life with us.

B. Show What You Know

Match the items in Column A with those in Column B.

Column A

1. justice
2. the Cross
3. obedience
4. fortitude

Column B

____ **a.** sign of Jesus' great love for his Father and us

____ **b.** strengthens us to respect people in authority

____ **c.** good habit of being fair and kind

____ **d.** strengthens us to do what is right and good when it is difficult

C. Connect with Scripture

What was your favorite story about Jesus in this unit? Draw something that happened in the story. Tell your class about it.

D. Be a Disciple

1. *What Saint or holy person did you enjoy hearing about in this unit? Write the name here. Tell your class what this person did to follow Jesus.*

_____

2. *What can you do to be a good disciple of Jesus?*

_____

_____

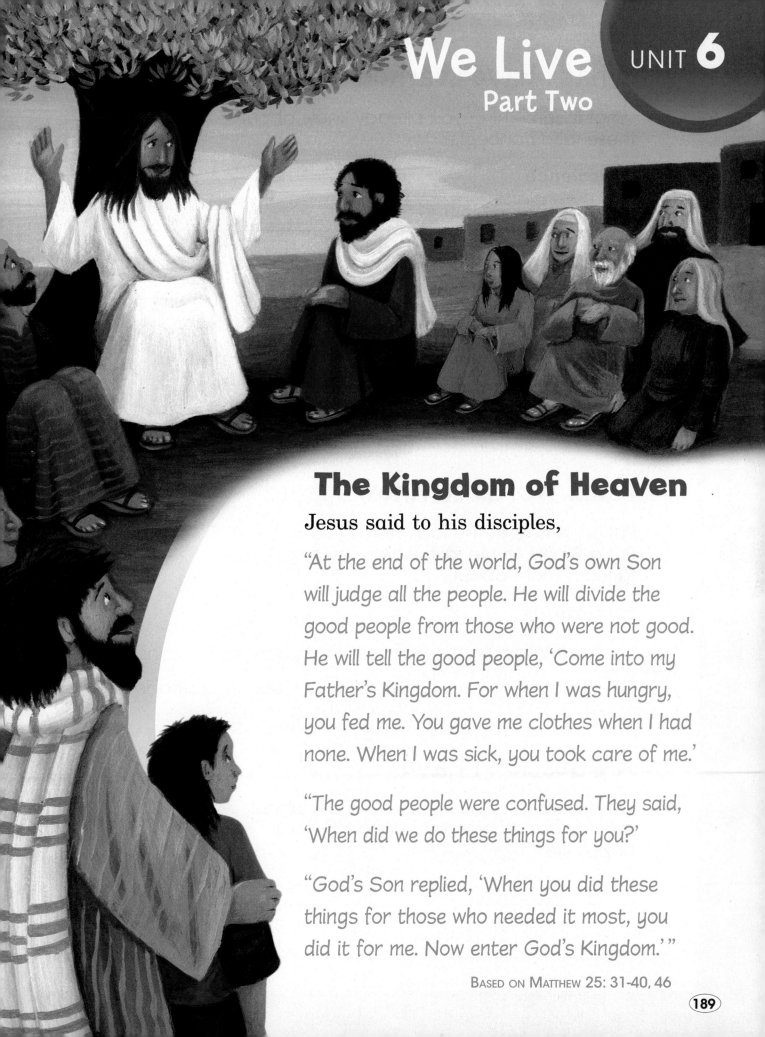

The Kingdom of Heaven

Jesus said to his disciples,

"At the end of the world, God's own Son will judge all the people. He will divide the good people from those who were not good. He will tell the good people, 'Come into my Father's Kingdom. For when I was hungry, you fed me. You gave me clothes when I had none. When I was sick, you took care of me.'

"The good people were confused. They said, 'When did we do these things for you?'

"God's Son replied, 'When you did these things for those who needed it most, you did it for me. Now enter God's Kingdom.'"

BASED ON MATTHEW 25: 31-40, 46

What I Have Learned

What is something you already know about these faith concepts?

conscience

_____

_____

the Our Father

_____

_____

Faith Words to Know

Put an **X** next to the faith words you know.
Put a **?** next to the faith words you need to learn more about.

Faith Words

____ mortal sin   ____ sanctifying grace   ____ consequences

____ Heaven   ____ Kingdom of God   ____ hope

A Question I Have

What question would you like to ask about making good choices to live a holy and happy life?

_____

_____

Chapter 21

We Make Choices

? What was a good choice you made recently?

Some of God's people were not following God's ways. Listen to what Joshua, a leader of God's people, told them they had to do.

Whom will you choose to serve? My family and I choose to serve the Lord our God.

BASED ON JOSHUA 24:15

? How can a family serve the Lord?

Disciple Power

Humility

Humility helps us to recognize that all we are and all we have comes from God. We are humble when we choose to follow God's ways and make them our own.

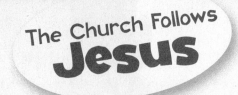

The Church Follows Jesus

Saint Francis of Assisi

We have to make choices about the way we want to live. Here is a story about someone who made many important choices.

Francis grew up thinking he would be happy by becoming a rich and famous soldier. So Francis set off to win battles.

But one night, Francis had a dream. In the dream, God asked Francis to return home. Francis chose to do what God asked.

Francis gave away all his riches and began to live a very simple and humble life. Francis chose to serve the Lord.

Today, we know Francis as Saint Francis of Assisi because that is where he lived. His followers are called Franciscans. Like Saint Francis, they choose poverty and to humbly serve the Lord.

? What was Saint Francis' choice?

Making Wise Choices

God sent Jesus to show us how to make **wise choices**. A wise choice is one that helps us live as God's children. Jesus always did what his Father asked him to do. We will be truly happy when we make choices as Jesus taught us.

God wants us to be happy now and forever in **Heaven**. Heaven is being happy with God and with all the Saints forever. Making wise choices now will help us find happiness in Heaven.

Faith Focus
Why is it important to make wise choices?

Faith Vocabulary
wise choices
Wise choices help us to live as children of God.

Heaven
Heaven is happiness forever with God and all the Saints.

Activity

Look and think about what is happening in these pictures. Tell what choice you would make next. Share why your choices are wise choices.

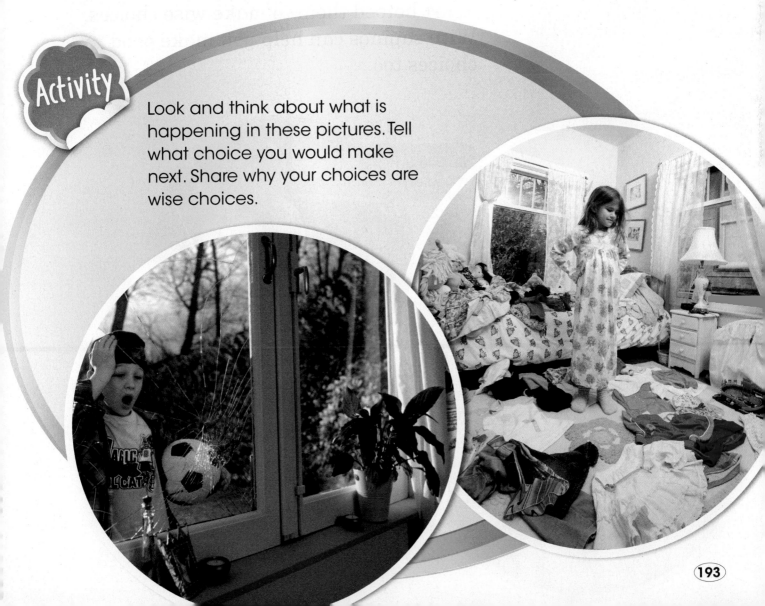

Clare was a dear friend of Saint Francis of Assisi. Like Francis, she chose to give up her riches and serve God. Clare gathered other women around her to live simple lives of service to others. Followers of Saint Clare are called Poor Clares. They live in convents and spend most of their days praying for others. The Church celebrates the feast of Saint Clare on August 11.

Wise Sayings

Wise sayings can help us make wise choices. Think of wise sayings you know, for example, "Buckle Up" or "Stop, Drop, and Roll."

You have learned that the Bible has many wise sayings called **proverbs**. Proverbs are short, wise sayings that help us to make wise choices. They help us to love God and to follow his commands.

Many of God's people in Old Testament times could not read or write. Listening very carefully and learning proverbs by heart helped them to make wise choices. Wise sayings can help you make good choices too.

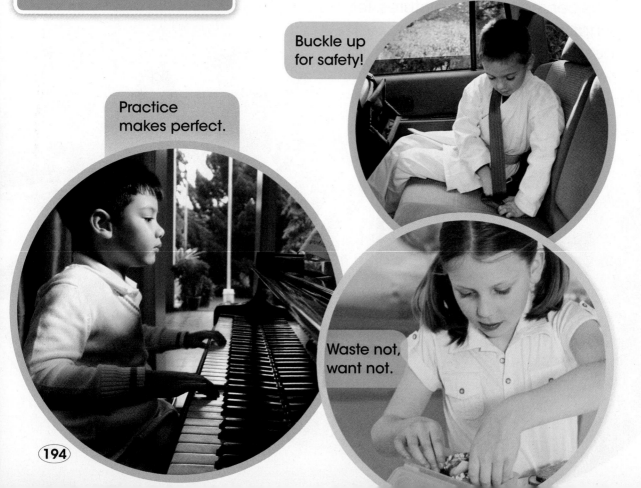

Buckle up for safety!

Practice makes perfect.

Waste not, want not.

Choosing Wisely

Remember, the proverbs in the Bible come from God. They helped God's people of long ago make good and wise choices. The proverbs can also help us make good and wise choices today.

Trust in the LORD,

and your plans will succeed.

BASED ON PROVERBS 16:3

Activity Draw lines to connect the children to the proverb from the Bible that will best help them choose wisely.

Maireni wonders if she should listen to her mom. Should she plan the best bus route to her friend's house or just go and hope she finds the right way.

Work hard and become a leader; be lazy and become a loser.
(Based on Proverbs 12:24)

Jake wants to be on the basketball team. He wonders, "Should I practice shooting baskets or just play video games?"

For the gloomy person, every day is sad; but for the cheerful person, every day is a delight.
(Based on Proverbs 15:15)

Ichiro wakes up, looks out the window, and wonders, "What will this day be like, happy or sad?"

Say no to good advice, and your plans will fail. Say yes to good advice, and your plans will succeed.
(Based on Proverbs 15:22)

I Follow Jesus

Remember that Jesus came to show you how to make wise choices. A wise saying in the Book of Proverbs reminds us, "Happy is the person who chooses to make peace" (based on Proverbs 12:20). You choose wisely when you choose to make peace.

Activity

My Proverb

Create a wise saying of your own. Help others to see why they should be humble.

_____

_____

_____

_____

_____

My Faith Choice

This week, I will choose to be a peacemaker by speaking kindly. I will remember to

_____

_____

Pray, "Dear Lord, help me grow in humility. Help me choose to serve you in peace. Amen."

Chapter Review

Two words are missing from each sentence. Use words in the box to complete the sentences.

happy	wise	proverbs
sayings	Heaven	choices

1. God wants us to be _____ now and forever in _____.

2. Wise _____ can help us make wise _____.

3. _____ from the Bible can help us make _____ choices today.

TO HELP YOU REMEMBER

1. It is important for us to make wise choices.

2. Making wise choices now will help us find happiness in Heaven.

3. The proverbs can help us choose wisely.

A Peace Prayer

Saint Francis of Assisi prayed that God would help him to be a peacemaker.

All — **Lord, make us instruments of your peace.**

Group 1 — Where there is hatred,

Group 2 — let us bring love.

Group 1 — Where there is injury,

Group 2 — let us bring forgiveness.

All — **Lord, make us instruments of your peace.**

BASED ON THE PRAYER OF SAINT FRANCIS

With My Family

This Week . . .

In Chapter 21, "We Make Choices," your child learned:

▶ God has created us to be happy now and forever with him in Heaven.

▶ The choices we make can lead us to or away from happiness in this world and the next.

▶ Proverbs are wise sayings in the Bible that help us make wise choices today.

▶ The virtue of humility helps us recognize that all our blessings and the blessings of others are from God.

For more about related teachings of the Church, see the *Catechism of the Catholic Church*, 1719–1724 and 2825; and the *United States Catholic Catechism for Adults*, pages 315–317.

Sharing God's Word

Read together Proverbs 12:24; 15:15; 15:23; and 16:3, or read the adaptation of these verses on page 195. Emphasize that the proverbs in the Bible can help us make wise choices about how to live as God's children.

We Live as Disciples

The Christian home and family is a school of discipleship. Choose one of the following activities to do as a family, or design a similar activity of your own:

▶ Choose one of the proverbs in this chapter. Tell how the proverb can help your family live and choose what is right and good. Make it a motto for your family this week. Place it on a card on your refrigerator so that the whole family can see it.

▶ When you make family decisions together, join first in humble prayer. Praying together before decision-making not only strengthens family ties but also helps your children grow in humility as they model the humility you show in seeking God's help through prayer.

Our Spiritual Journey

Our spiritual journey finds its end in Heaven. Throughout his ministry, Jesus was continually calling us to heaven. Pray the prayer of Saint Francis on page 197 this week. Your prayer may make all the difference in this world . . . and in the next.

For more ideas on ways your family can live as disciples of Jesus, visit **www.BeMyDisciples.com**

Chapter 22

We Can Choose Right from Wrong

? How do we know if a choice is right or wrong?

God wants you to choose for yourself. God also wants you to choose wisely. Listen to what God says in the Bible.

> God lets us choose right or wrong, life or death. Choose what is right. Choose life so that you can be happy with God forever.
>
> BASED ON DEUTERONOMY 30:19

? Why is it important to do what is right?

Joy

Joy is one of the Fruits of the Holy Spirit. Joy shows that we are thankful for God's love and for all that God has made. Joy shows that we enjoy life and delight in making others joyful.

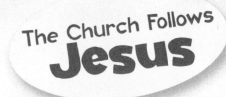

The Church Follows **Jesus**

Paula's Choice

Sometimes, the choices we make are simple ones. But even the simplest choice, if it is a wise choice, can make a big difference. It can bring happiness to us and to others.

When Paula Frassinetti was nine years old, her mother died. Who would take care of her younger brothers? Paula decided that she would.

Paula's choice meant a lot of work for her. She could not go to school. So her brothers shared with her what they learned in school. Paula chose to be cheerful. She went to Mass every day and prayed while she did her chores.

When Paula grew up, she opened a school for poor girls. She later founded a religious order to educate poor children.

The Church honors her today as Saint Paula. Her feast day is June 11.

❓ Which choices did Saint Paula make? Did her choices make anyone happy? Who?

Choosing Right from Wrong

Faith Focus
Why is it important to follow your conscience when making choices?

God lets us make choices for ourselves. We can choose to love God or not. We can choose to love others or not. In the Bible we read,

> When God created us, he gave us free choice. It is our choice to do or not to do God's will.

BASED ON SIRACH 15:14-15

Faith Vocabulary
▶ **consequences**
Consequences are the good or bad things that happen after we make choices.

▶ **conscience**
Conscience is a gift from God that helps us to make wise choices.

Things happen when we make choices. These good or bad things are called **consequences**. We are responsible for the consequences of our actions.

If we make a choice against God's Law, we sin. If we sin, we have to make up for the harm we do.

Activity

Read this story. Write what you think Sarah will do. Then draw what will happen next.

Sarah's Choice

Sarah's little sister Katie is sick. Sarah asks her parents, "May I read Katie a story?" But then a friend asks her to come over to play. What will Sarah do?

Saint Philip Neri

Philip Neri made wise choices. He sold all his possessions and gave away his money. He visited banks, shops, and places where people gathered. Every place he visited, he tried to convince people to serve God in all they did. The Church celebrates the feast day of Saint Philip Neri on May 26.

The Gift of Our Consciences

A wise choice is a good choice to live as Jesus taught. God gives us a gift that helps us to make good choices. This gift is called *conscience*.

Our consciences tell us whether a choice we have made, or are about to make, is right or wrong.

Conscience is like a compass. It points us in the right direction. It shows us the way to goodness. It leads the way to happiness.

Activity

Read each statement and think about your day. Circle the happy and sad faces to help you to review the choices you have made today.

Thinking About Our Choices

1. I prayed to God to ask for help.

2. I showed my love to family members.

3. I showed my love to my friends.

4. I showed my love to other people.

Training Our Consciences

Making wise choices is very important. We make good choices when we know right from wrong. We learn right from wrong from our family. We learn from the good example of others. We learn from God's rules of love. We learn from the teaching and example of Jesus and from the teaching of the Church.

When we learn and remember what is right or wrong, we are forming our consciences. Then our consciences can help us make good choices. Making good choices makes good things happen. Making good choices makes us happy.

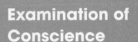

Activity

Let Conscience Be Your Guide

These four steps can help you listen to your conscience and make a wise choice.

1. **Think:** What are the possible choices?

2. **Consider:** What might happen next?

3. **Ask:** What does your conscience tell you is the best choice to make?

4. **Act:** Follow your conscience and make the good choice.

Read the sentence below. Then follow the steps to a decision of good conscience.

Your friend is angry, makes fun of you, and calls you a name. You feel hurt and upset.

What do you do?
Act out your choice for your class.

I Follow Jesus

A wise choice is a choice to live as Jesus taught. Your conscience helps you to know right from wrong. Your conscience helps you make wise choices.

Activity

Making Choices

Circle the pictures that show children making a good choice to live as Jesus taught. Write an X on the pictures that show a bad choice. Explain your answers!

My Faith Choice

I can choose to make choices to live with joy as Jesus taught. This week, I will

_____

_____

 Pray, "Holy Spirit, help me listen to my conscience. Let me do what is right and pleasing to you. Amen."

Chapter Review

Unscramble the letters to make a word you learned in this chapter. Write a sentence using the word. Share your sentence with others.

S C I C O N E N C E

C __ __ **S C** __ __ **N** __ __ __

_____

_____ .

> **TO HELP YOU REMEMBER**

> 1. We are making wise choices when we choose to live as Jesus taught.

> 2. Wise choices show we are forming and following our consciences.

> 3. All of our choices have consequences.

Be the Joy of My Heart

Saint Augustine chose to change his life and to follow Jesus. His choice brought him great happiness. This is his prayer. Pray it with joy.

O God,
Be the light of my life.
Be the life of my soul.
Be the strength of my mind.
Help me choose what is right.
Keep me always in your love.
Be the joy of my heart.
Amen.

BASED ON A PRAYER OF SAINT AUGUSTINE

With My Family

This Week . . .

In Chapter 22, "We Can Choose Right from Wrong," your child learned:

▶ We are responsible for the choices we make and for their consequences.

▶ God has given us the gift of a conscience to help us discern right from wrong.

▶ We have the responsibility to form a good conscience to help us live according to God's will.

▶ A well-formed conscience leads to decisions that bring happiness here and in Heaven.

▶ The gift of joy urges us to choose what makes for happiness.

For more about related teachings of the Church, see the *Catechism of the Catholic Church*, 1716–1724, 1730–1738, and 1776–1794, and the *United States Catholic Catechism for Adults*, pages 314–315 and 341–369.

■ Sharing God's Word

Read together Sirach 15:14-15 or read the adaptation of these verses on page 201. Emphasize that God created us with free will and the ability to make our own choices.

■ We Live as Disciples

The Christian home and family is a school of discipleship. Choose one of the following activities to do as a family, or design a similar activity of your own:

▶ When you watch a TV show together, point out when characters on the show make good choices and when they make bad choices. If someone makes a bad choice, make suggestions for a good choice.

▶ Talk about the choices family members made during the day and their consequences. Such a discussion will get your child started thinking about his or her responsibility for the consequences of his or her choices.

■ Our Spiritual Journey

We learn to exercise our free will by practicing discernment. We do so by calling on the Holy Spirit to lead or give direction regarding the choices we make. Discernment can open the door to a new way of life—to a life of joy in the Spirit. Pray "Be the Joy of My Heart" on page 205. Encourage your child to ask for guidance in making decisions.

For more ideas on ways your family can live as disciples of Jesus, visit **www.BeMyDisciples.com**

Chapter 23

We Share in God's Life

? Tell about a special gift that you have received. What made this gift so special?

Grace helps us to live holy lives. Listen to what the Bible tells us about grace.

Jesus is the living Word of God. He is God's own Son, full of grace and truth. From Jesus, we receive grace and more grace.

BASED ON JOHN 1:14, 16

? Who helps you to live a holy life?

Trust

When we trust people, we know we can rely on them. We can depend on them to help us when we are in need.

The Church Follows **Jesus**

A Caring Ministry

Most people in prison have made decisions that hurt others and themselves. Still, God gives the gift of grace to them through people who care for them.

Jesus tells us that caring for people like prisoners is the same as caring for him.

> [I was] in prison and you visited me.
>
> MATTHEW 25:36

Prison chaplains are trained to care for people in prison. They bring the love of Christ to them. The prisoners know they can trust them.

Sister Natalie Rossi, a Sister of Mercy, works at a women's prison in Pennsylvania. Sister Natalie and prison chaplains like her show prisoners that God still loves them. The prisoners know they can trust her. She helps them see that God loves them even though they did wrong.

? How do prison chaplains like Sister Natalie help people in prison to be open to God's grace?

Amazing Grace

Sister Natalie helped others understand that the gift of God's grace is offered to all people.

God also helps us to live as his children. The Holy Spirit always gives us the grace to make wise choices.

God has given us the gift of **sanctifying grace**. The word *sanctifying* means "something that makes us holy." We first receive this gift in Baptism.

The gift of sanctifying grace makes us children of God. God shares his life with us. God's grace makes us holy.

Faith Focus
What does the gift of grace help us to do?

Faith Vocabulary
sanctifying grace
Sanctifying grace is the gift of God sharing his life with us.

Activity

Color the X's one color. Color the O's different colors. Thank God for the wonderful gift of grace.

209

Saint Monica

Monica's son was Augustine. When Augustine was young, he often made unwise choices. Monica prayed that her son would make better choices. He did and lived a holy life. Today the Church honors them as Saints. The Church celebrates the feast day of Saint Monica on August 27.

Living a Holy Life

It is not always easy to choose to live a holy life. Sometimes we choose to sin. All sins hurt our relationships with God and other people. Some sins are very serious. We call these sins mortal sins. When we commit serious sins, we lose the gift of sanctifying grace.

We need to confess our serious sins in the Sacrament of Penance and Reconciliation. When we are sorry for our sins and confess them in this Sacrament, God forgives our sins. We receive the gift of sanctifying grace again. We are filled with God's life. We receive God's grace to live a holy life. We are at peace.

? What are some of the ways you can show you are truly sorry for your sins?

Jesus Brings Peace

After his Resurrection, Jesus' first word and last gift to his disciples was *peace*.

"Peace be with you," Jesus said to his disciples. "The Father sent me. Now I send you." Then Jesus breathed on them, saying, "Receive the Holy Spirit."

BASED ON JOHN 20:22

Peace is Jesus' final, grace-filled gift to us. The gift of peace comes from knowing we are living as friends of God and people.

The Holy Spirit brings us God's peace. The Holy Spirit gives us the help we need to remain in God's grace.

When we are at peace, we are loving God above all else and loving others as we love ourselves. We are living the Great Commandment. We are living the life of grace.

Activity

When we gather to celebrate Mass, we share the gift of peace with one another. Draw yourself sharing a sign of peace.

I Follow Jesus

God shares the gift of his life with us. Jesus gives us the gift of peace. The Holy Spirit helps us to live as children of God. One way you can live as a child of God is to be a peacemaker. When you show compassion for others, you bring them peace.

Activity

Signs of Peace

Work with your teacher or parent. Create a message that tells how people your age can live as peacemakers.

_____

_____

_____

_____

_____

My Faith Choice

This week, I will be a person whom others can trust. I will

_____

_____.

Pray, "Thank you, Holy Spirit, for helping me to live as a peacemaker. Amen."

Chapter Review

Choose three words from the list that show ways we can live peaceful and holy lives. Write a sentence using the words you choose.

sin	grace	care	compassion	anger

_____

_____

_____

► **TO HELP YOU REMEMBER**

1. Grace is a gift from God.

2. Sanctifying grace is the gift of God's life that he shares with us.

3. The gift of peace helps us live holy and happy lives.

The Hail Mary

Learn the Hail Mary by heart. Pray it every day to show your love for Mary. Ask Mary to help you bring peace to others.

Group 1 Hail, Mary, full of grace, the Lord is with thee.

Group 2 Blessed art thou among women and blessed is the fruit of thy womb, Jesus.

All **Holy Mary, Mother of God, pray for us sinners, now and at the hour of our death. Amen.**

With My Family

This Week . . .

In Chapter 23, "We Share in God's Life," your child learned:

► God shares divine life with us in the gift of sanctifying grace.

► God calls us to live holy lives.

► Sin turns us away from God's love and deters us from living holy lives.

► Sharing the gift of peace is crucial for living a holy and happy life.

► Compassion and trust are virtues that helps us care about and for others.

For more about related teachings of the Church, see the *Catechism of the Catholic Church*, 1846–1869 and 1996–2016, and the *United States Catholic Catechism for Adults*, pages 193 and 328–330.

Sharing God's Word

Read together John 1:14, 16. Emphasize that through Jesus, we receive the God-given gift of divine help, or grace, to live as children of God.

We Live as Disciples

The Christian home and family is a school of discipleship. Choose one of the following activities to do as a family, or design a similar activity of your own:

► Help your children create peace place mats. Use the place mats at family meals as reminders to share meals in peace and to be peacemakers for one another. Discuss situations where you can show compassion.

► Point out to your child the many ways your family is "graced." Show your child how to count blessings and so live a holy, happy, and peace-filled life.

Our Spiritual Journey

Catholics look upon Mary as the purest of creatures, not subject to the slavery that sin imposes. Catholics believe that Mary is totally graced, totally responsive to the divine will, and totally faithful. God comes to Mary seeking her consent. Mary's "yes" joins the creature to God in the work of completing the labors of creation. Help your child learn the great prayer to Mary, the Hail Mary (page 213). Use it for your family prayer this week.

For more ideas on ways your family can live as disciples of Jesus, visit **www.BeMyDisciples.com**

Chapter 24

The Our Father

? Who first taught you how to pray? What is your favorite prayer?

Jesus' disciples wanted to know the best way to pray. Jesus taught them:

"This is how you are to pray: Our Father in heaven, hallowed be your name." MATTHEW 6:9

? Do you know the name of the prayer Jesus taught?

Hope

Hope is trusting that God hears us, cares about us, and will care for us.

The Church Follows Jesus

A Life of Prayer

The Our Father is the prayer of the whole Church. Catholics all over the world pray the Our Father every day.

Some people in the Church do more than pray every day. They pray all day long. They believe God has called them to pray always. Convents, abbeys, and monasteries are three of the places where these praying people live. Saint Benedict was one of these praying people.

These people remind us that God is the Father of all people. They trust that God our Father loves us and cares for us. They pray for the Church and for the whole world.

Activity

Work with a partner. Which problems in your neighborhood or in the world would you like to pray for? List them here.

_____

_____

_____

The Our Father

The Our Father helps us to pray to God and understand how to live as his children.

Our Father, who art in heaven

God is the Father of all people. God creates us in his image and likeness. God shares his life and love with us now and forever.

Hallowed be thy name

The word *hallowed* means "very holy." We love God above all else. We adore and worship God. We honor and respect the name of God in all we say and do.

Thy kingdom come

Jesus announced the coming of the **Kingdom of God**. The Kingdom of God is also called the Kingdom of Heaven. When we love God above all else, we live as Jesus taught. We prepare for the coming of the Kingdom of God in its fullness.

❓ What are the things you do and say that show your love for God the Father?

Faith Focus
Why do we pray the Our Father?

Faith Vocabulary
Kingdom of God
The Kingdom of God is also called the Kingdom of Heaven. It is people and creation living in friendship with God.

Faith-Filled People

Saint Thomas Aquinas

Thomas lived more than 700 years ago. Thomas became a Dominican priest. He wrote an important book about God. Saint Thomas called the Lord's Prayer the "most perfect of prayers."

Thy will be done on earth as it is in heaven

We pray that all will do God's will. The Holy Spirit helps us to continue the work of Jesus. We share God's love with our family, friends, and everyone we meet.

Give us this day our daily bread

We always trust God. God knows what we need. We ask God to help us to live as his children. We pray for all people to receive God's blessings.

Activity

Draw lines to connect each part of the Our Father to its meaning.

Our Father.	We say God's holy name with love.
who art in heaven,	God's love for us is now and forever.
hallowed be thy name;	God is the Father of all.
thy kingdom come,	The Kingdom of God is called Heaven.
thy will be done on earth as it is in heaen	God gives us what we need.
Give us this day our daily bread,	We continue the work of Jesus.

Forgive us our trespasses, as we forgive those who trespass against us

Jesus taught us to be forgiving persons. Asking for forgiveness and forgiving others helps us to live as children of God and followers of Jesus.

Lead us not into temptation, but deliver us from evil

We ask God to help us to say no to temptation. Temptation is everything that can lead us away from God's love. The Holy Spirit will help us.

Amen

We end our prayer by saying, "Amen." *Amen* means "Yes, it is true. We believe!"

Activity

Draw lines to connect each part of the Our Father to its meaning.

and forgive us our trespasses, as we forgive those who trespass against us;	We ask God to protect us.
	We believe!
and lead us not into temptation,	We ask God to help us to choose what is good.
but deliver us from evil.	
Amen.	God forgives us as we forgive others.

I Follow Jesus

The Holy Spirit is helping you to live the Our Father now. He is helping you to grow in hope. He is helping you to live as a member of the family of God's people.

Activity

A Disciple of Jesus

Put a ✔ next to some ways you could try to live the words of the Our Father this summer. Make a plan to put your choice into action.

_____ Pray.

_____ Make wise choices.

_____ Forgive those who hurt me.

_____ Say I am sorry when I hurt someone else.

_____ Listen to the Holy Spirit, who helps me to make wise choices.

My Faith Choice

I will live the Our Father. This week, I will do one of the things I checked. I will continue to do the things I checked all summer. I will

_____.

Pray, "Thank you, Holy Spirit, for helping me to live the Our Father. Amen."

Chapter Review

Choose the right word to complete each sentence.

Temptation	**pray**	**Kingdom**
Father	**Hallowed**	

1. _____ means "very holy."

2. When you _____, you lift up your heart to God.

3. God is our _____.

4. _____ is something that leads us away from God.

5. Living as God wants us to live helps us to prepare for

   the _____ of God.

TO HELP YOU REMEMBER

1. We pray the Our Father to show our love and adoration of God.

2. The Our Father helps us to live as children of God.

3. The Our Father helps us to prepare for the Kingdom of God.

Go Forth!

Jesus taught that we must live our faith in God. Thank God for all you learned this year. Live your faith in Jesus and make a difference. Be his disciple!

Leader Lord, each day we will remember to act like children of God.

All **Thanks be to God!**

Leader Lord, we will love and serve you every day.

All **Thanks be to God!**

Leader Lord, we will treat others with kindness and bring them hope.

All **Thanks be to God!**

With My Family

This Week . . .

In Chapter 24, "The Our Father," your child learned:

▶ Jesus taught his disciples how to pray by teaching them the Our Father.

▶ The Our Father helps us to understand how to live as God's children.

▶ The virtue of hope is trusting that God will always act on our behalf.

▶ When we pray the Our Father, we discover what it means to live as children of God and to prepare for the coming of the Kingdom of God.

For more about related teachings of the Church, see the *Catechism of the Catholic Church*, 2777–2856, and the *United States Catholic Catechism for Adults*, pages 481–492.

■ Sharing God's Word

Read together Matthew 6:9-13, where Jesus teaches the Our Father. Emphasize that the Our Father is not only a prayer, it is a "summary of the whole Gospel." Praying the Our Father teaches us how to pray and how to live as children of God.

■ We Live as Disciples

The Christian home and family is a school of discipleship. Choose one of the following activities to do as a family, or design a similar activity of your own:

▶ Make an Our Father booklet. As you read each part of the Our Father, write the words of that part in your booklet. Write or draw how you can live each part of the Our Father.

▶ Talk about some of the ways your family lives the Our Father. Pray to the Holy Spirit. Ask the Holy Spirit to help your family live the Our Father each day.

▶ As a family, discuss and list reasons why Christians are a people of hope.

■ Our Spiritual Journey

"**Go in peace**, glorifying the Lord by your life." These words, from the Dismissal in the *Roman Missal*, send us forth from Mass. They challenge us to live a life worthy of being children of God. Praying the Our Father daily not only reminds us who we are—children of a heavenly Father—but also reminds us to offer glory to God. Be sure that your children memorize the Our Father. It is part of their Christian identity. Pray it together daily.

For more ideas on ways your family can live as disciples of Jesus, visit **www.BeMyDisciples.com**

Unit 6 Review

Name _____

A. Choose the Best Word

Complete the sentences. Color the circle next to the best choice for each sentence.

1. Our consciences tell us whether a choice we are going to make is a _____ one.

○ fun   ○ sad   ○ wise or bad

2. God's gift of sanctifying _____ makes us holy and children of God.

○ love   ○ help   ○ grace

3. A very serious sin is called a _____ sin.

○ mortal   ○ sanctifying ○ venial

4. Jesus taught his disciples the _____.

○ Hail Mary   ○ Sign of the Cross   ○ Our Father

5. The Kingdom of _____ is all people living as God wants them to live.

○ Saints   ○ God   ○ Earth

B. Show What You Know

Color the box to mark the sentences that are true.

❑ Proverbs can help us make wise choices.

❑ We are not free to choose to do what is right or what is wrong.

❑ Jesus taught us to pray to God the Father.

❑ Another name for the Our Father is the Jesus Prayer.

C. Connect with Scripture

What was your favorite story about Jesus in this unit? Draw something that happened in the story. Tell your class about it.

D. Be a Disciple

1. *What Saint or holy person did you enjoy hearing about in this unit? Write the name here. Tell your class what this person did to follow Jesus.*

_____

2. *What can you do to be a good disciple of Jesus?*

_____

_____

The Year of Grace

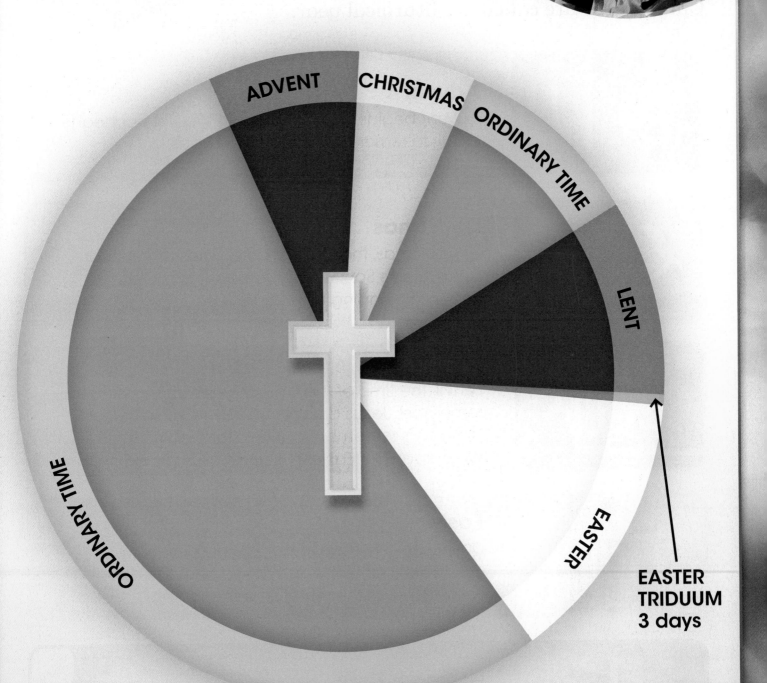

ADVENT

CHRISTMAS

ORDINARY TIME

LENT

EASTER

EASTER
TRIDUUM
3 days

ORDINARY TIME

The Liturgical Year

The Church celebrates her faith all year long in prayer and worship. The seasons of the Church year are called the liturgical year.

Advent

Advent begins the Church year. We get our hearts ready to remember the birth of Jesus.

Christmas

At Christmas, the Church celebrates the birth of Jesus, God's Son. We praise and thank God the Father for sending us his Son, Jesus.

Lent

Lent is the time of the Church year when we remember Jesus died for us. We make sacrifices to help us remember our love for God and others. We prepare for Easter.

Easter

During the fifty days of the Easter season, we celebrate that Jesus was raised from the dead. Jesus gave us the gift of new life.

Ordinary Time

Ordinary Time is the longest time of the Church year. We learn to live as followers of Jesus.

Faith Focus
What do the
Saints show us?

**The Word
of the Lord**
This is the second
reading for the
Solemnity of All
Saints. Ask your
family to read
it with you. Talk
about the reading
with them.

Second reading
1 John 3:1-3

All Saints

Just as there are members of our family who help us make right choices, there are members of our Church family who show us how to follow Jesus. The people are called Saints. They are holy people who love God very much. They live in Heaven with Jesus and see the glory of God.

The Church honors all Saints who live with God in heaven by setting aside a special feast day. We call this the Solemnity of All Saints. It is celebrated on November 1. We go to Mass and thank God for the Saints in Heaven and for their help.

We believe the Saints ask God to help us. They help us to live holy lives as children of God.

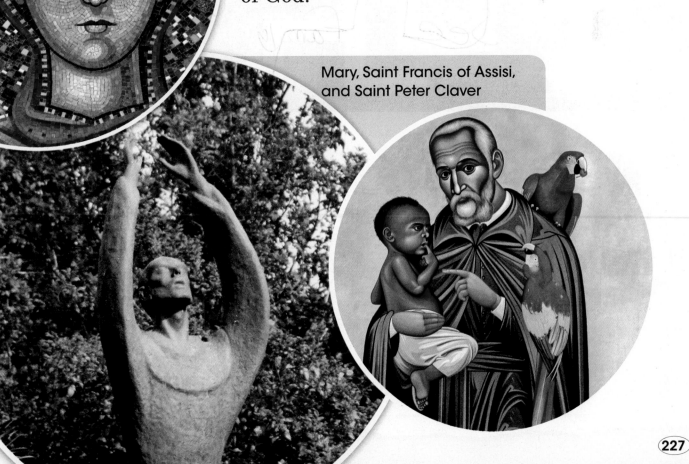

Mary, Saint Francis of Assisi, and Saint Peter Claver

Following Jesus

The Saints show us how to live as followers of Jesus. Draw yourself next to the Saint below. Draw a line along the path that will take you to Jesus.

This week, I will live as a faithful follower of Jesus. I will

_____

_____

 Pray, "Thank you, Lord, for the holy men, women, and children who teach us to love you. Amen."

Faith Focus
How does the Church celebrate her special love for Mary, the Mother of God?

The Word of the Lord
This is the Gospel reading for the Solemnity of the Immaculate Conception. Ask your family to read it with you. Talk about the reading with them.

Luke 1:26-38

Immaculate Conception

God has a very special love for Mary. The Church has a special love for Mary too. God chose Mary to be the Mother of Jesus, the Son of God. God prepared Mary to be Jesus' mother in a very special way.

God gave Mary a very special grace, or gift. Mary was always free from sin. Mary was born without sin. Mary received God's help all through her life so she would never commit a sin. We call this help from God "grace."

The angel Gabriel came to Mary to tell her that God had chosen her to be the Mother of his Son. This is what the angel said,

"Hail Mary, full of grace, the Lord is with you."

BASED ON LUKE 1:30

We call this special grace the Immaculate Conception of Mary. We celebrate the Solemnity of the Immaculate Conception every year on December 8. We honor Mary and her special role as the Mother of Jesus, the Savior of the world.

This day is also a holy day of obligation. This means that Catholics have the responsibility to take part in the celebration of Mass. In this way, we honor God and thank him for the special grace he gave Mary.

Thank You, Mary

In this space, create a thank-you card to Mary. Write a message. Draw a picture. Thank Mary for saying yes to God. Thank her for her prayers and for helping you make good choices.

This week, I will honor Mary. I will follow the example of Mary, the Mother of Jesus. I will

_____

_____.

Pray, "Mary, God loves you. I love you too. Blessed are you among all women! Amen."

Faith Focus
Why did the angels visit the shepherds?

The Word of the Lord
This is the Gospel reading for Mass on Christmas. Ask your family to read it with you. Talk about the reading with them.

Years A, B, and C
Luke 2:1-14 (Mass at Midnight)

What You See
The Christmas tree is made up of evergreens. It reminds us that God always loves us.

Christmas

Sometimes people tell us good news. Angels told good news to shepherds. They told the shepherds the good news of the birth of Jesus.

The angels praised God for this good news. They sang,

"Glory to God in the highest and on earth peace to those on whom his favor rests."

LUKE 2:14

At Mass, we sing this great song of the angels. We call it the "Gloria." We use their words to sing, "Glory to God in the highest, and on earth peace to people of good will."

235

Give Glory to God

Color in the letters of this prayer. Pray the prayer each day of the Christmas season when you wake up. Pray it again at bedtime.

GLORY to GOD!

My Faith Choice

This week, I will honor the angels. I will follow their example of telling others about Jesus. I will

_____

_____

Pray, "Jesus, you are the Light of the world. Let your light shine everywhere. Amen."

Faith Focus
How does the Church honor Mary, Mother of God?

The Word of the Lord
This is the Gospel reading for the Solemnity of Mary, Mother of God. Ask your family to read the Gospel reading with you. Talk about the reading with them.

Gospel
Luke 2:16-21

Mary, the Holy Mother of God

Mother's Day is a special day set aside to honor our mothers. We make a special effort to let our mothers know how much we love them. Sometimes we make our moms special cards. We want to thank our moms for loving us.

During the Christmas season on January 1, we honor Mary. On this day, we celebrate that Mary was blessed by God. She was chosen to be the Mother of Jesus, God's Son. Through the power of the Holy Spirit, the Blessed Virgin Mary became the Mother of Jesus.

We honor Mary, the Mother of God, by going to Mass. We praise God for the gift of Jesus, his Son. We thank God for the gift of Mary, the Mother of God. We ask Mary, our Blessed Mother, to pray for us.

Mary Mosaic. Cartagena de Indias, Colombia

We Thank You, Mary!

Create a Mother's Day card for Mary. Address
the card and ask Mary for her help and
guidance. Don't forget to sign your name!

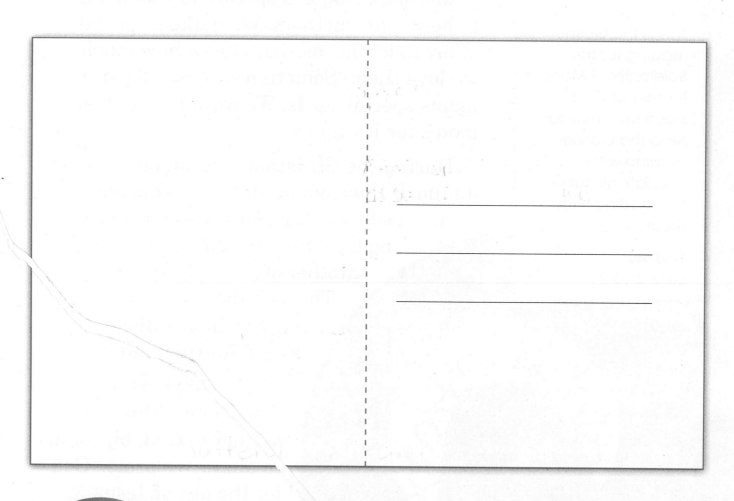

 My Faith Choice

This week, I will be like Mary, the Mother of God. I will
show my love for God by

_____

_____ .

 Pray, "Most loving Mother, Mary, pray for me to the
Lord, our God. Amen."

Faith Focus
How did the Magi honor Jesus?

The Word of the Lord
This is the Gospel reading for the feast of the Epiphany. Ask your family to read it with you. Talk about the reading with them.

Years A, B, and C
Matthew 2:1-12

Epiphany

We all like to receive gifts. When someone gives us a gift, they are showing us they love us. Long ago, some wise people called Magi gave special gifts to the newborn Jesus.

The Magi saw a bright star in the night sky. They believed that the star was telling them about the birth of a newborn king. The Magi left their homes. They followed the star and traveled many miles to Bethlehem. There they found Jesus with Mary and Joseph. Bowing low, they gave Jesus gifts of gold, frankincense, and myrrh.

The Magi came a long way to honor Jesus. The Gospel story of the Magi reminds us that Jesus welcomes everyone who comes to him.

The Savior of the World

Pretend you are with the Magi on their journey. Follow the maze to Jesus. What gift would you bring to Jesus? What would you say to Jesus when you give your gift to him?

This week, I will follow the example of the Magi. I will

_____

_____

Pray, "Jesus, King of kings, always guide us to you. Amen."

Faith Focus
How do we begin the celebration of Lent?

The Word of the Lord
This is the Gospel reading for Ash Wednesday. Ask your family to read it with you. Talk about the reading with them.

Gospel
Matthew 6:1-6, 16-18

Ash Wednesday

Easter is the celebration of the Resurrection. We celebrate the rising of Jesus from the dead to new life. At Baptism, we receive new life in Jesus too. We share in his Resurrection.

During Lent, we prepare our hearts and minds to celebrate Easter. We remember our Baptism. We make choices to live our Baptism better. Ash Wednesday is the first day of Lent.

We prepare for Easter during Lent by fasting, praying, and doing good things for others. When we go to church on Ash Wednesday, we pray, "A clean heart create for me, O God." We ask God to help us make good choices to live our Baptism. We pray so our hearts will be ready for Jesus.

On Ash Wednesday, the sign of the cross is made in ashes on our foreheads. Catholics all over the world wear this cross to show they love God and want to live their Baptism. They want to live as good and faithful disciples of Jesus.

Prayer for Forgiveness

In the Act of Contrition, we tell God we are sorry for our sins. Praying this prayer is one way we can ask for God's forgiveness. Fill in the blanks to complete the prayer.

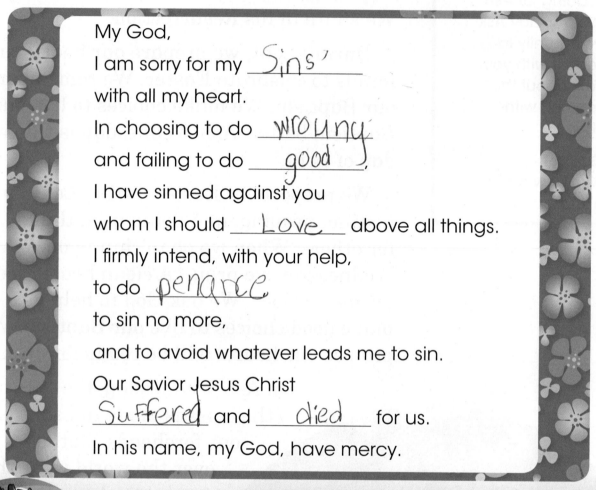

My God,

I am sorry for my _Sins'_ with all my heart.

In choosing to do _wrong,_ and failing to do _good_,

I have sinned against you

whom I should _Love_ above all things.

I firmly intend, with your help,

to do _penance,_

to sin no more,

and to avoid whatever leads me to sin.

Our Savior Jesus Christ

Suffered and _died_ for us.

In his name, my God, have mercy.

My Faith Choice

This week, I will try to memorize the Act of Contrition. I will ask my family to help me. (Circle the time you will pray.)

† Every morning
† Every afternoon
† Every evening

Pray, "Help me during Lent, Lord, to become more like Jesus. Amen."

Faith Focus
How does celebrating Lent help us to get ready for Easter?

The Word of the Lord
These are Gospel readings for the First Sunday of Lent. Ask your family to read this year's Gospel reading with you. Talk about the reading with them.

Year A
Matthew 4:1-11

Year B
Mark 1:12-15

Year C
Luke 4:1-13

What You See
During Lent, the Church uses the color purple or violet. The colors purple and violet remind us of sorrow and penance.

Lent

Sometimes a special day seems far away. But we can do many things to get ready for that day.

During Lent, we do many things to get ready to celebrate Easter. Lent is forty days long. It begins on Ash Wednesday. During Lent, we turn to God and pray each day. We make sacrifices by giving up some things. This helps us to show our love for God and others.

Lent is the special time of the year the Church prepares new members for Baptism. It is the time members of the Church prepare to renew the promises we made at Baptism.

We do all these things during Lent to help us to prepare for Easter. Easter is a special day for all Christians. It is the day of Jesus' Resurrection.

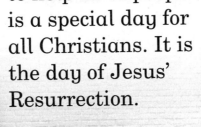

Prepare for Easter

Pick a partner. Take turns answering each question.
Decide how to keep Lent and prepare for Easter.
On the lines, write your answers to each question.

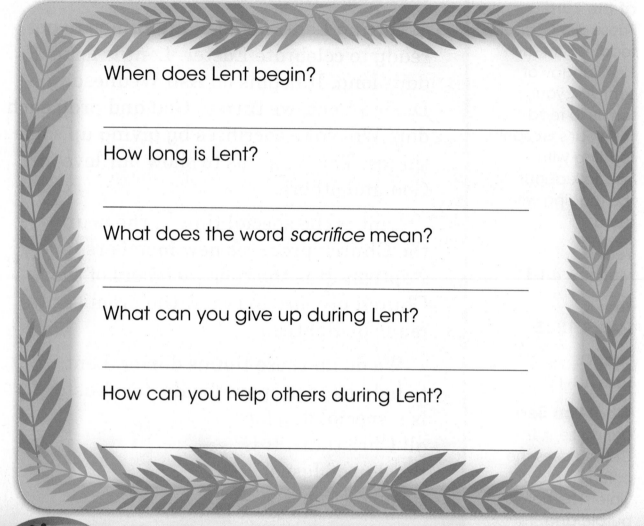

When does Lent begin?

_____

How long is Lent?

_____

What does the word *sacrifice* mean?

_____

What can you give up during Lent?

_____

How can you help others during Lent?

_____

This Lent, I will prepare for Easter. I will

_____

_____.

 Pray, "Jesus, help me to show my love for God and others. Amen."

Faith Focus
How do we begin our celebration of Holy Week?

The Word of the Lord
These are the Gospel readings for Palm Sunday of the Lord's Passion. Ask your family to read this year's Gospel reading with you. Talk about the reading with them.

Year A
Matthew 26: 14-27: 66
or Matthew 27:11–54

Year B
Mark 14:1-15:47
or Mark 15:1-39

Year C
Luke 22:14-23:56
or Luke 23:1-49

What You See
We carry palm branches in procession. We hold them as we listen to the Gospel reading.

Palm Sunday of the Passion of the Lord

When friends come to visit, we welcome them. Once when Jesus came to visit Jerusalem, many people came out to welcome him. They spread cloaks and branches on the road to honor him. The Church remembers and celebrates that special time on Palm Sunday of the Lord's Passion. It is the first day of Holy Week. Holy Week is the week before Easter.

At Mass on Palm Sunday, we honor Jesus. We hold palm branches and say, "Hosanna to the Son of David. Blessed is he who comes in the name of the Lord!" We welcome Jesus as the people welcomed him to Jerusalem.

We Honor Jesus

People sometimes carry banners in processions. Sometimes we hang banners in our church. Banners in our church help us to remember the liturgical season or feast we are celebrating. Decorate this banner.

"Blessed is he who comes in the name of the Lord!"

This Holy Week, I will welcome Jesus. I will

_____

_____.

Pray, "Blessed are you, Lord Jesus. Hosanna!"

Triduum/Holy Thursday

Faith Focus
How does celebrating Holy Thursday help us to grow as followers of Jesus Christ?

The Word of the Lord
These are the Scripture readings for the Mass of the Lord's Supper on Holy Thursday. Ask your family to read one of the readings with you. Talk about the reading with them.

First Reading
Exodus 12:1-8, 11-14

Second Reading
1 Corinthians 11:23-26

Gospel
John 13:1-15

What You See
The priest washes the feet of members of the parish. This reminds us that we are to help others as Jesus taught us.

Many things happen at a family meal. We prepare and cook food. We set the table. We clean up. When we do all these things, we are serving one another.

On Holy Thursday, we remember how Jesus showed his love by serving his disciples. Before Jesus and his disciples ate the meal at the Last Supper, he washed their feet. After he finished, he told them to serve others as he served them.

On Holy Thursday, we remember all Jesus did at the Last Supper. We especially remember that Jesus gave us the Eucharist.

Prayer for Holy Thursday

The hymn "Where Charity and Love Are Found" is sung in many churches on Holy Thursday. The words of this hymn remind us that God is love. We are to love one another as Jesus loved us. Pray this prayer with your class.

Child 1   The love of Christ gathers us.

All   **Where charity and love are found, there is God.**

Child 2   Let us be glad and rejoice in him.

All   **Where charity . . .**

Child 3   Let us love each other deep in our hearts.

All   **Where charity . . .**

Child 4   Let all people live in peace.

My Faith Choice

For one day, I will serve like Jesus served. I will

_____

_____

Pray, "Lord Jesus, help me to serve others as you did. Amen."

Faith Focus
How does celebrating Good Friday help us to grow as followers of Christ?

The Word of the Lord
These are the Scripture readings for Good Friday. Ask your family to read the readings with you. Talk about each reading with them.

First Reading
Isaiah 52:13-53:12

Second Reading
Hebrews 4:14-16, 5:7-9

Gospel
John 18:1-19:42

Triduum/Good Friday

Sometimes something happens to us that brings us suffering. We call this a cross. On Good Friday, we remember that Jesus died on the Cross. We listen to the story of his Passion and Death. We pray for everyone in the world.

On Good Friday, we honor the Cross by kissing it or by genuflecting or bowing deeply in front of it. Our celebration of Jesus' Passion and Death ends with the Communion Service. We walk in procession to the altar and share in the Eucharist. We receive the Body of Christ.

At home we think about how Jesus suffered and died on this day. Our prayers help us to get ready for the joy of Jesus' new life at Easter.

Prayers for the Whole World

On Good Friday, the Church prays a special Prayer of the Faithful. Pray this prayer of the faithful together:

Child 1   May God guide our Church and gather us in peace.

All   **Amen.**

Child 2   May God help the Pope to lead us as God's holy people.

All   **Amen.**

Child 3   May God help those who will soon be baptized to follow Jesus.

All   **Amen.**

Child 4   May God bless our government leaders and help them keep us safe and free.

All   **Amen.**

Child 5   May God fill those in need with faith and hope.

All   **Amen.**

BASED ON THE SOLEMN INTERCESSIONS,
THE PASSION OF THE LORD, ROMAN MISSAL

On this day, I will honor the Cross. I will

_____

_____

Pray, "We adore you, O Christ, and we bless you."

Triduum/Easter Sunday

Faith Focus
Why is Easter the most important season of the Church year?

The Word of the Lord
These are the Gospel readings for Easter Sunday. Ask your family to read the Gospel reading for this year with you. Talk about it with them.

Year A
John 20:1-9
or Matthew 28:1-10
or Luke 24:13-35

Year B
John 20:1-9
or Mark 16:1-7
or Luke 24:13-35

Year C
John 20:1-9
or Luke 24:1-12
or Luke 24:13-35

What is the best day of your life? Why do you say it is the best day you remember? For Christians, Easter is the best day of all days. On this day God raised Jesus from death.

During Easter, we remember that we are one with Jesus Christ, who is risen. For Christians, every Sunday is a little Easter. Sunday is the Lord's Day. It is the day on which Jesus was raised from death to new life.

Easter and every Sunday are days of joy and celebration. On these days, we remember that through Baptism we share in his new life now and forever.

Celebrating Our New Life

The Earth is filled with signs that remind us of the gift of new life in Christ we receive in Baptism. Find and color the signs of new life in this drawing. Talk with your family about what the signs you discover tell about Easter.

On this day, I will honor the Resurrected Christ. I will rejoice in his new life. I will

_____

_____

 Pray, "Christ is risen! Alleluia!"

Ascension of the Lord

After Jesus rose from the dead, he continued to teach his Apostles. He reminded them that soon he would leave them to be with his Father in Heaven. Jesus promised the Apostles that he would send the Holy Spirit to them.

Forty days after Easter, Jesus and the Apostles were in the countryside. He told them that the Holy Spirit would help them to share his teachings with people all over the world.

Jesus raised his hands and blessed the Apostles. Then he was lifted up into heaven. The Apostles returned to Jerusalem to wait for the coming of the Holy Spirit.

BASED ON LUKE 24:50-53

The Church celebrates Jesus' return to his Father in Heaven on the Solemnity of the Ascension of the Lord, forty days after Easter (or on the Seventh Sunday of Easter.) Jesus promised to prepare a place for us in Heaven. We rejoice that one day we too will share in the glory of Heaven with Jesus and all the Saints.

An Ascension Prayer

When Jesus rose from the dead and returned
to his Father, he showed us the way to Heaven.
We rejoice in the Resurrection and the Ascension.

Child 1 Jesus, you rose from the dead.

All **We celebrate your new life. Alleluia!**

Child 2 Jesus, you promised to send the Holy Spirit.

All **You are with us always. Alleluia!**

Child 3 Jesus, you ascended to your Father in Heaven.

All **You will come again in glory to bring us to our heavenly home. Alleluia!**

My Faith Choice

I can prepare for everlasting life in Heaven by living as a disciple as Jesus asks. I will

_____

_____.

Pray, "Jesus, show us the way to Heaven. Alleluia!"

Faith Focus
Who helps us to live as followers of Jesus?

The Word of the Lord
These are the Scripture readings for Pentecost. Ask your family to read one of the readings with you. Talk about the reading with them.

First Reading
Acts 2:1-11

Second Reading
1 Corinthians 12:3-7, 12-13

Gospel
John 20:19-23

Pentecost Sunday

What do you do when you have to do something that is very difficult? How do you feel when someone helps you?

Jesus knew it would not be easy for his disciples to do the work he gave them. So he promised that the Holy Spirit would come and help them.

On the day of Pentecost, the Holy Spirit came to Peter the Apostle and the other disciples as Jesus promised. Peter was filled with courage. He told a crowd from many different countries that God had raised Jesus to new life. Everyone was amazed by what Peter was saying. Over 3,000 people became followers of Jesus that day.

The Holy Spirit is our helper and teacher too. The Holy Spirit helps us to tell others about Jesus and teaches us to live as followers of Jesus.

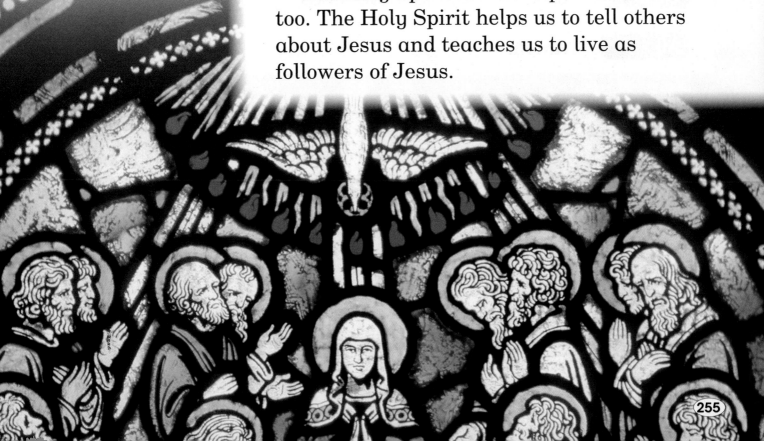

Come, Holy Spirit

The Holy Spirit helps us to live as followers of Jesus. Unscramble the scrambled words in each sentence of this prayer. Write the missing letters of the words on the lines under each sentence. Pray the prayer to the Holy Spirit together.

All   **Come, Holy Spirit, be our guest, in our work,**

be our (ster).   r _____ ____ t

Group 1   When we are hurt, (lhea) us.   h _____ _____ l

Group 2   When we are weak, make us (torsng).

_____ _____ _____ **ong**

Group 1   When we fail, (whas) our sins away.   w _____ s _____

Group 2   Bring us (jyo) that never ends.   _____ _____ y

All   **Amen.**

My Faith Choice

Like the disciples, I will tell others about Jesus with the help of the Holy Spirit. I will

_____

_____ .

Pray, "Come, Holy Spirit, come! Guide us to God!"

Catholic Prayers and Practices

Sign of the Cross

In the name of the Father,
and of the Son,
and of the Holy Spirit. Amen.

Our Father

Our Father, who art in heaven,
hallowed be thy name;
thy kingdom come,
thy will be done
on earth as it is in heaven.
Give us this day our daily bread,
and forgive us our trespasses,
as we forgive those who trespass
  against us;
and lead us not into temptation,
  but deliver us from evil.
Amen.

Glory Be (Doxology)

Glory be to the Father
and to the Son
and to the Holy Spirit,
as it was in the beginning
is now, and ever shall be
world without end. Amen.

The Hail Mary

Hail, Mary, full of grace,
the Lord is with thee.
Blessed art thou among women
and blessed is the fruit
  of thy womb, Jesus.
Holy Mary, Mother of God,
pray for us sinners,
now and at the hour of our death.
Amen.

Signum Crucis

In nómine Patris,
et Fílii,
et Spíritus Sancti. Amen.

Pater Noster

Pater noster, qui es in cælis:
sanctificétur nomen tuum;
advéniat regnum tuum;
fiat volúntas tua,
  sicut in cælo, et in terra.
Panem nostrum cotidiánum
  da nobis hódie;
et dimítte nobis débita nostra,
sicut et nos dimíttimus debitóribus
  nostris;
et ne nos indúcas in tentatiónem;
sed líbera nos a malo. Amen.

Gloria Patri

Glória Patri
et Fílio
et Spirítui Sancto.
Sicut erat in princípio,
et nunc et semper
et in sæcula sæculórum. Amen.

Ave, Maria

Ave, María, grátia plena,
Dóminus tecum.
Benedícta tu in muliéribus,
et benedíctus fructus ventris tui,
  Iesus.
Sancta María, Mater Dei,
ora pro nobis peccatóribus,
nunc et in hora mortis nostræ.
Amen.

Apostles' Creed

(from the *Roman Missal*)

I believe in God,
the Father almighty,
Creator of heaven and earth,
and in Jesus Christ, his only Son,
   our Lord,

*(At the words that follow, up to and
including the Virgin Mary, all bow.)*

who was conceived by the Holy Spirit,
born of the Virgin Mary,
suffered under Pontius Pilate,
was crucified, died and was buried;
he descended into hell;
on the third day he rose again from
   the dead;
he ascended into heaven,
and is seated at the right hand of
   God the Father almighty;
from there he will come to judge the
   living and the dead.
I believe in the Holy Spirit,
the holy catholic Church,
the communion of saints,
the forgiveness of sins,
the resurrection of the body,
and life everlasting. Amen.

Nicene Creed

(from the *Roman Missal*)

I believe in one God,
the Father almighty,
maker of heaven and earth,
of all things visible and invisible.

I believe in one Lord Jesus Christ,
the Only Begotten Son of God,
born of the Father before all ages.

God from God, Light from Light,
true God from true God,
begotten, not made, consubstantial
   with the Father;
through him all things were made.
For us men and for our salvation
he came down from heaven,

*(At the words that follow, up to and
including* and became man, *all bow.)*

and by the Holy Spirit was incarnate
   of the Virgin Mary,
and became man.

For our sake he was crucified under
   Pontius Pilate,
he suffered death and was buried,
and rose again on the third day
in accordance with the Scriptures.
He ascended into heaven
and is seated at the right hand of
   the Father.
He will come again in glory
to judge the living and the dead
and his kingdom will have no end.

I believe in the Holy Spirit, the Lord,
   the giver of life,
who proceeds from the Father and
   the Son,
who with the Father and the Son is
   adored and glorified,
who has spoken through the prophets.

I believe in one, holy, catholic and
   apostolic Church.
I confess one Baptism for the
   forgiveness of sins
and I look forward to the resurrection
   of the dead
and the life of the world to come. Amen.

Morning Prayer

Dear God,
as I begin this day,
keep me in your love and care.
Help me to live as your child today.
Bless me, my family, and my friends
   in all we do.
Keep us all close to you. Amen.

Grace Before Meals

Bless us, O Lord,
   and these thy gifts,
which we are about to receive
   from thy bounty,
      through Christ our Lord.
Amen.

Grace After Meals

We give thee thanks,
   for all thy benefits, almighty God,
who lives and reigns forever. Amen.

Evening Prayer

Dear God,
I thank you for today.
Keep me safe throughout the night.
Thank you for all the good I did today.
I am sorry for what I have chosen
   to do wrong.
Bless my family and friends. Amen.

A Vocation Prayer

God, I know you will call me
for special work in my life.
Help me follow Jesus each day
and be ready to answer your call.
Amen.

Act of Contrition

My God,
I am sorry for my sins
   with all my heart.
In choosing to do wrong
and failing to do good,
I have sinned against you
whom I should love above all things.
I firmly intend, with your help,
to do penance,
to sin no more,
and to avoid whatever leads me
   to sin.
Our Savior Jesus Christ
suffered and died for us.
In his name, my God, have mercy.
Amen.

Rosary

Catholics pray the Rosary to honor Mary and remember the important events in the lives of Jesus and Mary. There are twenty mysteries of the Rosary. Follow the steps from 1 to 5.

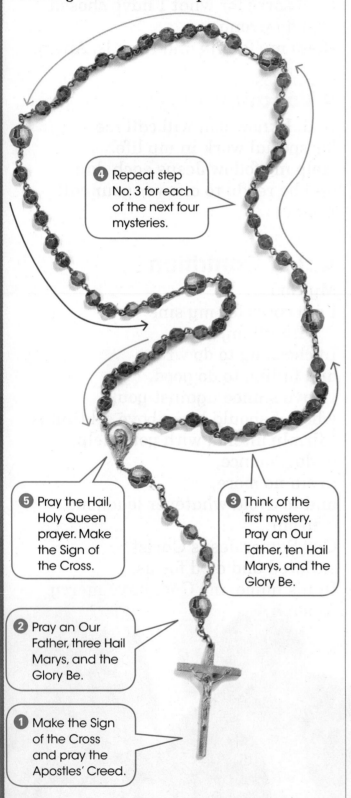

4 Repeat step No. 3 for each of the next four mysteries.

5 Pray the Hail, Holy Queen prayer. Make the Sign of the Cross.

3 Think of the first mystery. Pray an Our Father, ten Hail Marys, and the Glory Be.

2 Pray an Our Father, three Hail Marys, and the Glory Be.

1 Make the Sign of the Cross and pray the Apostles' Creed.

Joyful Mysteries

1. The Annunciation
2. The Visitation
3. The Nativity
4. The Presentation in the Temple
5. The Finding the Child of Jesus After Three Days in the Temple

Luminous Mysteries

1. The Baptism of Jesus at the Jordan
2. The Miracle at Cana
3. The Proclamation of the Kingdom and the Call to Conversion
4. The Transfiguration
5. The Institution of the Eucharist

Sorrowful Mysteries

1. The Agony in the Garden
2. The Scourging at the Pillar
3. The Crowning with Thorns
4. The Carrying of the Cross
5. The Crucifixion and Death

Glorious Mysteries

1. The Resurrection
2. The Ascension
3. The Descent of the Holy Spirit at Pentecost
4. The Assumption of Mary
5. The Crowning of the Blessed Virgin as Queen of Heaven and Earth

Hail, Holy Queen

Hail, holy Queen, Mother of mercy: Hail, our life, our sweetness, and our hope. To you do we cry, poor banished children of Eve. To you do we send up our sighs, mourning and weeping in the valley of tears. Turn, then, most gracious advocate, your eyes of mercy toward us; and after this our exile show unto us the blessed fruit of your womb, Jesus. O clement, O loving, O sweet Virgin Mary.

The Ten Commandments

1. I am the LORD your God: you shall not have strange gods before me.
2. You shall not take the name of the LORD your God in vain.
3. Remember to keep holy the LORD's Day.
4. Honor your father and your mother.
5. You shall not kill.
6. You shall not commit adultery.
7. You shall not steal.
8. You shall not lie.
9. You shall not covet your neighbor's wife.
10. You shall not covet your neighbor's goods.

Based on Exodus 20:2-3, 7-17

Precepts of the Church

1. Participate in Mass on Sundays and holy days of obligation, and rest from unnecessary work.
2. Confess sins at least once a year.
3. Receive Holy Communion at least during the Easter season.
4. Observe the prescribed days of fasting and abstinence.
5. Provide for the material needs of the Church, according to one's abilities.

The Great Commandment

"You shall love the Lord, your God, with all your heart, with all your soul, and with all your mind. . . . You shall love your neighbor as yourself." Matthew 22:37, 39

The Law of Love

"This is my commandment: love one another as I love you."

John 15:12

The Seven Sacraments

Jesus gave the Church the Seven Sacraments. The Seven Sacraments are signs of God's love for us. When we celebrate the Sacraments, Jesus is really present with us. We share in the life of the Holy Trinity.

Baptism

We are joined to Christ. We become members of the Body of Christ, the Church.

Confirmation

The Holy Spirit strengthens us to live as children of God.

Eucharist

We receive the Body and Blood of Jesus.

Penance and Reconciliation

We receive God's gift of forgiveness and peace.

Anointing of the Sick

We receive God's healing strength when we are sick or dying, or weak because of old age.

Holy Orders

A baptized man is ordained to serve the Church as a bishop, priest, or deacon.

Matrimony

A baptized man and a baptized woman make a lifelong promise to love and respect each other as husband and wife. They promise to accept the gift of children from God.

We Celebrate the Mass

The Introductory Rites

We remember that we are the community
of the Church. We prepare to listen to the Word of God
and to celebrate the Eucharist.

The Entrance

We stand as the priest, deacon, and other ministers enter the assembly. We sing a gathering song. The priest and deacon kiss the altar. The priest then goes to the chair, where he presides over the celebration.

Sign of the Cross and Greeting

The priest leads us in praying the Sign of the Cross. The priest greets us, and we say,

"And with your spirit."

The Penitential Act

We admit our wrongdoings. We bless God for his mercy.

The Gloria

We praise God for all the good that he has done for us.

The Collect

The priest leads us in praying the Collect. We respond, "Amen."

The Liturgy of the Word

God speaks to us today.
We listen and respond to God's Word.

The First Reading from Scripture

We sit and listen as the reader reads from the Old Testament or from the Acts of the Apostles. The reader concludes, "The word of the Lord." We respond,

"Thanks be to God."

The Responsorial Psalm

The song leader leads us in singing a psalm.

The Second Reading from Scripture

The reader reads from the New Testament, but not from the four Gospels. The reader concludes, "The word of the Lord." We respond,

"Thanks be to God."

The Acclamation

We stand to honor Christ, present with us in the Gospel. The song leader leads us in singing **"Alleluia, Alleluia, Alleluia,"** or another chant during Lent.

The Gospel

The deacon or priest proclaims, "A reading from the holy Gospel according to (name of Gospel writer)." We respond,

"Glory to you, O Lord."

He proclaims the Gospel. At the end he says, "The Gospel of the Lord." We respond,

"Praise to you, Lord Jesus Christ."

The Homily

We sit. The priest or deacon preaches the homily. He helps the people gathered to understand the Word of God spoken to us in the readings.

The Profession of Faith

We stand and profess our faith. We pray the Nicene Creed together.

The Prayer of the Faithful

The priest leads us in praying for our Church and her leaders, for our country and its leaders, for ourselves and others, for those who are sick and those who have died. We can respond to each prayer in several ways. One way that we respond is,

"Lord, hear our prayer."

The Liturgy of the Eucharist

We join with Jesus and the Holy Spirit
to give thanks and praise to God the Father.

The Preparation of the Gifts

We sit as the altar table is prepared
and the collection is taken up.
We share our blessings with the
community of the Church and
especially with those in need. The
song leader may lead us in singing
a song. The gifts of bread and wine
are brought to the altar.

The priest lifts up the bread and
blesses God for all our gifts. He
prays, "Blessed are you, Lord God of
all creation. . . ." We respond,

"Blessed be God for ever."

The priest lifts up the cup of wine
and prays, "Blessed are you, Lord
God of all creation. . . . " We respond,

"Blessed be God for ever."

The priest invites us,
"Pray, brothers and sisters,
that my sacrifice and yours
may be acceptable to God,
the almighty Father."

We stand and respond,
**"May the Lord accept the
sacrifice at your hands for
the praise and glory of his
name, for our good, and the
good of all his holy Church."**

The Prayer over the Offerings

The priest leads us in praying the
Prayer over the Offerings.
We respond, **"Amen**."

Opening Dialogue and Preface

The priest invites us to join in praying the Church's great prayer of praise and thanksgiving to God the Father.

Priest: "The Lord be with you."

Assembly: "And with your spirit."

Priest: "Lift up your hearts."

Assembly: "We lift them up to the Lord."

Priest: "Let us give thanks to the Lord our God."

Assembly: "It is right and just."

After the priest sings or prays aloud the Preface, we join in acclaiming,

> **"Holy, Holy, Holy Lord God of hosts.**
> **Heaven and earth are full of your glory.**
> **Hosanna in the highest.**
> **Blessed is he who comes in the name of the Lord.**
> **Hosanna in the highest."**

The Eucharistic Prayer

The priest leads the assembly in praying the Eucharistic Prayer. We call on the Holy Spirit to make so gifts of bread and wine holy so that they become the Body and Blood of Jesus. We recall what happened at the Last Supper. The bread and wine become the Body and Blood of the Lord. Jesus is truly and really present under the appearances of bread and wine.

The priest sings or says aloud, "The mystery of faith." We respond using this or another acclamation used by the Church,

> **"We proclaim your Death, O Lord, and profess your Resurrection until you come again."**

The priest then prays for the Church. He prays for the living and the dead.

Doxology

The priest concludes the praying of the Eucharistic Prayer. He sings or prays aloud,

> "Through him, and with him, and in him,
> O God, almighty Father,
> in the unity of the Holy Spirit, all glory and honor is yours,
> for ever and ever."

We respond by singing, **"Amen."**

The Communion Rite

The Lord's Prayer
We pray the Lord's Prayer together.

The Sign of Peace
The priest invites us to share a sign of peace, saying, "The peace of the Lord be with you always." We respond,

"And with your spirit."

We share a sign of peace.

The Fraction, or the Breaking of the Bread
The priest breaks the host, the consecrated bread. We sing or pray aloud,

"Lamb of God, you take away the sins of the world,
    have mercy on us.
Lamb of God, you take away the sins of the world,
    have mercy on us.
Lamb of God, you take away the sins of the world,
    grant us peace."

Communion
The priest raises the host and says aloud,

"Behold the Lamb of God,
behold him who takes away the
    sins of the world.
Blessed are those called to the
    supper of the Lamb."

We join with him and say,

"Lord, I am not worthy that you should enter under my roof, but only say the word and my soul shall be healed."

The priest receives Communion. Next, the deacon and the extraordinary ministers of Holy Communion and the members of the assembly receive Communion.

The priest, deacon, or extraordinary minister of Holy Communion holds up the host. We bow, and the priest, deacon, or extraordinary minister of Holy Communion says, "The Body of Christ." We respond, "**Amen**." We then receive the consecrated host in our hands or on our tongues.

If we are to receive the Blood of Christ, the priest, deacon, or extraordinary minister of Holy Communion holds up the cup containing the consecrated wine. We bow, and the priest, deacon, or extraordinary minister of Holy Communion says, "The Blood of Christ." We respond, "**Amen**." We take the cup in our hands and drink from it.

The Prayer After Communion
We stand as the priest invites us to pray, saying, "Let us pray." He prays the Prayer After Communion. We respond,

"Amen."

The Concluding Rites

We are sent forth to do good works, praising and blessing the Lord.

Greeting

We stand. The priest greets us as we prepare to leave. He says, "The Lord be with you." We respond, **"And with your spirit."**

Final Blessing

The priest or deacon may invite us, "Bow your heads and pray for God's blessing."
The priest blesses us, saying, "May almighty God bless you: the Father, and the Son, and the Holy Spirit."
We respond, **"Amen."**

Dismissal of the People

The priest or deacon sends us forth, using these or similar words, "Go in peace, glorifying the Lord by your life."
We respond, **"Thanks be to God."**
We sing a hymn. The priest and the deacon kiss the altar. The priest, deacon, and other ministers bow to the altar and leave in procession.

The Sacrament of Penance and Reconciliation

Individual Rite

Greeting
Scripture Reading
Confession of Sins
   and Acceptance of Penance
Act of Contrition
Absolution
Closing Prayer

Communal Rite

Greeting
Scripture Reading
Homily
Examination of Conscience, a
   Litany of Contrition, and the
   Lord's Prayer
Individual Confession and Absolution
Closing Prayer

Key Teachings of the Catholic Church

The Mystery of God

Divine Revelation

Who am I?

You are a person created by God. God wants you to live in friendship with him on Earth and forever in Heaven.

How do we know this about ourselves?

God knows and loves all people. God wants us to know and love him too. God tells us about ourselves. God also tells us about himself.

How did God tell us?

God tells us in many ways. First, all the things God has created tell us about him. We see God's goodness and beauty in creation. Second, God came to us and he told us about himself. He told us the most when he sent his Son, Jesus Christ. God's Son became one of us and lived among us. He showed us who God is.

What is faith?

Faith is a gift from God. It helps us to know and to believe in God.

What is a mystery of faith?

A mystery of faith can never be known completely. We cannot know everything about God. We only know who God is because he told us about himself.

What is Divine Revelation?

God wants us to know about him. Divine Revelation is how he freely makes himself known to us. God has told us about himself and his plan for us. He has done this so that we can live in friendship with him and with one another forever.

What is Sacred Tradition?

The word *tradition* means "to pass on." The Church's Sacred Tradition passes on what God has told us. The Holy Spirit guides the Church to tell us about God.

Sacred Scripture

What is Sacred Scripture?

Sacred Scripture means "holy writings." Sacred Scripture are writings that tell God's story.

What is the Bible?

The Bible is God's Word. It is a holy book. The stories in the Bible teach about God. The Bible tells the stories about Jesus. When you listen to the Bible, you are listening to God.

What does it mean to say that the Bible is inspired?

This means that the Holy Spirit helped people write about God. The Holy Spirit helped the writers tell what God wants us to know about him.

What is the Old Testament?

The Old Testament is the first part of the Bible. It has forty-six books. They were written before the birth of Jesus. The Old Testament tells the story of creation. It tells about Adam and Eve. It tells about the promise, or Covenant, between God and his people.

What is the Covenant?

The Covenant is the promise that God and his people freely made. It is God's promise always to love and be kind to his people.

What are the writings of the prophets?

God chose people to speak in his name. These people are called the prophets. We read the message of the prophets in the Bible. The prophets remind God's people that God is faithful. They remind God's people to be faithful to the Covenant.

What is the New Testament?

The New Testament is the second part of the Bible. It has twenty-seven books. These books were inspired by the Holy Spirit. They were written during the time of the Apostles. They are about Jesus Christ. They tell about his saving work.

What are the Gospels?

The Gospels are the four books at the beginning of the New Testament. They tell the story of Jesus and his teachings. The four Gospels are Matthew, Mark, Luke, and John.

What are the letters of Saint Paul?

The letters of Saint Paul are in the New Testament. The letters teach about the Church. They tell how to follow Jesus. Some of these letters were written before the Gospels.

The Holy Trinity

Who is the Mystery of the Holy Trinity?

The Holy Trinity is the mystery of One God in Three Persons—God the Father, God the Son, and God the Holy Spirit.

Who is God the Father?

God the Father is the First Person of the Holy Trinity.

Who is God the Son?

God the Son is Jesus Christ. He is the Second Person of the Holy Trinity. God the Father sent his Son to be one of us and live with us.

Who is God the Holy Spirit?

The Holy Spirit is the Third Person of the Holy Trinity. God sends us the Holy Spirit to help us to know and love God better. The Holy Spirit helps us live as children of God.

Divine Work of Creation

What does it mean to call God the Creator?

God is the Creator. He has made everyone and everything out of love. He has created everyone and everything without any help.

Who are angels?

Angels are spiritual beings. They do not have bodies like we do. Angels give glory to God at all times. They sometimes serve God by bringing his message to people.

Why are human beings special?

God creates every human being in his image and likeness. God shares his life with us. God wants us to be happy with him forever.

What is the soul?

The soul is the spiritual part of a person. The soul will never die. It is the part of us that lives forever. It bears the image of God.

What is free will?

Free will is the power God gives us to choose between good and evil. Free will gives us the power to turn toward God.

What is Original Sin?

Original Sin is the sin of Adam and Eve. They chose to disobey God. As a result of Original Sin, death, sin, and suffering came into the world.

Jesus Christ, Son of God, Son of Mary

What is the Annunciation?

At the Annunciation, the angel Gabriel came to Mary. The angel had a message for her. God had chosen her to be the Mother of his Son, Jesus.

What is the Incarnation?

The Incarnation is the Son of God becoming a man and still being God. Jesus Christ is true God and true man.

What does it mean that Jesus is Lord?

The word *lord* means "master or ruler." When we call Jesus "Lord," we mean that he is truly God.

What is the Paschal Mystery?

The Paschal Mystery is the Passion, Death, Resurrection, and Ascension of Jesus Christ. Jesus passed over from death into new and glorious life.

What is Salvation?

The word *salvation* means "to save." It is the saving of all people from sin and death through Jesus Christ.

What is the Resurrection?

The Resurrection is God's raising Jesus from the dead to new life.

What is the Ascension?

The Ascension is the return of the Risen Jesus to his Father in Heaven.

What is the Second Coming of Christ?

Christ will come again in glory at the end of time. This is the Second Coming of Christ. He will judge the living and the dead. This is the fulfillment of God's plan.

What does it mean that Jesus is the Messiah?

The word *messiah* means "anointed one." He is the Messiah. God promised to send the Messiah to save all people. Jesus is the Savior of the world.

The Mystery of the Church

What is the Church?

The word *church* means "those who are called together." The Church is the Body of Christ. It is the new People of God.

What does the Church do?

The Church tells all people the Good News of Jesus Christ. The Church invites all people to know, love, and serve Jesus.

What is the Body of Christ?

The Church is the Body of Christ on Earth. Jesus Christ is the Head of the Church and all baptized people are its members.

Who are the People of God?

The Church is the People of God. God invites all people to belong to the People of God. The People of God live as one family in God.

What is the Communion of Saints?

The Communion of Saints is all of the holy people that make up the Church. It is the faithful followers of Jesus on Earth. It is those who have died who are still becoming holier. It is also those who have died and are happy forever with God in Heaven.

What are the Marks of the Church?

There are four main ways to describe the Church. We call these the four Marks of the Church. The Church is one, holy, catholic, and apostolic.

Who are the Apostles?

The Apostles were the disciples whom Jesus chose. He sent them to preach the Gospel to the whole world in his name. Some of their names are Peter, Andrew, James, and John.

What is Pentecost?

Pentecost is the day the Holy Spirit came to the disciples of Jesus. This happened fifty days after the Resurrection. The work of the Church began on this day.

Who are the clergy?

The clergy are bishops, priests, and deacons. They have received the Sacrament of Holy Orders. They serve the whole Church.

What is the work of the Pope?

Jesus Christ is the true Head of the Church. The Pope and the bishops lead the Church in his name. The Pope is the bishop of Rome. He is the successor to Saint Peter the Apostle, the first Pope. The Pope brings the Church together. The Holy Spirit guides the Pope when he speaks about faith and about what Catholics believe.

What is the work of the bishops?

The other bishops are the successors of the other Apostles. They teach and lead the Church in their dioceses. The Holy Spirit always guides the Pope and all of the bishops. He guides them when they make important decisions.

What is religious life?

Some men and women want to follow Jesus in a special way. They choose the religious life. They promise not to marry. They dedicate their whole lives to doing Jesus' work. They promise to live holy lives. They promise to live simply. They share what they have with others. They live together in groups and they promise to obey the rules of their community. They may lead quiet lives of prayer, teach, or take care of people who are sick or poor.

Who are laypeople?

Many people do not receive the Sacrament of Holy Orders. Many are not members of a religious community. These are laypeople. Laypeople follow Christ every day by what they do and say.

The Blessed Virgin Mary

Who is Mary?

God chose Mary to be the Mother of his only Son, Jesus. Mary is the Mother of God. She is the Mother of Jesus. She is the Mother of the Church. Mary is the greatest Saint.

What is the Immaculate Conception?

From the first moment of her being, Mary was preserved from sin. This special grace from God continued throughout her whole life. We call this the Immaculate Conception.

What is the Assumption of Mary?

At the end of her life on Earth, the Blessed Virgin Mary was taken body and soul into Heaven. Mary hears our prayers. She tells her Son what we need. She reminds us of the life that we all hope to share when Christ, her Son, comes again in glory.

What is eternal life?

Eternal life is life after death. At death, the soul leaves the body. It passes into eternal life.

What is Heaven?

Heaven is living with God and with Mary and all the Saints in happiness forever after we die.

What is the Kingdom of God?

The Kingdom of God is also called the Kingdom of Heaven. It is all people and creation living in friendship with God.

What is Purgatory?

Purgatory is the chance to grow in love for God after we die so we can live forever in heaven.

What is Hell?

Hell is life away from God and the Saints forever after death.

Celebration of the Christian Life and Mystery

What is worship?

Worship is the praise we give God. The Church worships God in the liturgy.

What is liturgy?

The liturgy is the Church's worship of God. It is the work of the Body of Christ. Christ is present by the power of the Holy Spirit.

What is the liturgical year?

The liturgical year is the name of the seasons and feasts that make up the Church year of worship. The main seasons of the Church year are Advent, Christmas, Lent, and Easter. The Triduum is the three holy days just before Easter. The rest of the liturgical year is called Ordinary Time.

What are the Sacraments?

The Sacraments are the seven signs of God's love for us that Jesus gave the Church. We share in God's love when we celebrate the Sacraments.

What are the Sacraments of Christian Initiation?

The Sacraments of Christian Initiation are Baptism, Confirmation, and Eucharist.

What is the Sacrament of Baptism?

Baptism joins us to Christ. It makes us members of the Church. We receive the gift of the Holy Spirit. Original Sin and our personal sins are forgiven. Through Baptism, we belong to Christ.

What is the Sacrament of Confirmation?

At Confirmation, we receive the gift of the Holy Spirit. The Holy Spirit strengthens us to live our Baptism.

What is the Sacrament of Eucharist?

In the Eucharist, we join with Christ. We give thanksgiving, honor, and glory to God the Father. Through the power of the Holy Spirit, the bread and wine become the Body and Blood of Jesus Christ.

Why do we have to participate at Sunday Mass?

Catholics participate in the Eucharist on Sundays and holy days of obligation. Sunday is the Lord's Day. Participating at the Mass and receiving Holy Communion, the Body and Blood of Christ, when we are old enough, are necessary for Catholics.

What is the Mass?

The Mass is the main celebration of the Church. At Mass, we worship God. We listen to God's Word. We celebrate and share in the Eucharist.

What are the Sacraments of Healing?

The two Sacraments of Healing are the Sacrament of Penance and Reconciliation and the Sacrament of the Anointing of the Sick.

What is confession?

Confession is telling our sins to a priest in the Sacrament of Penance and Reconciliation. Confession is another name for this Sacrament.

What is contrition?

Contrition is being truly sorry for our sins. We want to make up for the hurt our sins have caused. We do not want to sin again.

What is penance?

A penance is a prayer or act of kindness. The penance we do shows that we are truly sorry for our sins. The priest gives us a penance to help repair the hurt caused by our sin.

What is absolution?

Absolution is the forgiveness of sins by God through the words and actions of the priest.

What is the Sacrament of the Anointing of the Sick?

The Sacrament of the Anointing of the Sick is one of the two Sacraments of Healing. We receive this Sacrament when we are very sick, old, or dying. This Sacrament helps make our faith and trust in God strong.

What are the Sacraments at the Service of Communion?

Holy Orders and Matrimony, or Marriage, are the two Sacraments at the Service of Communion. People who receive these Sacraments serve God.

What is the Sacrament of Holy Orders?

In this Sacrament, baptized men are consecrated as bishops, priests, or deacons. They serve the whole Church. They serve in the name and person of Christ.

Who is a bishop?

A bishop is a priest. He receives the fullness of the Sacrament of Holy Orders. He is a successor to the Apostles. He leads and serves in a diocese. He teaches and leads worship in the name of Jesus.

Who is a priest?

A priest is a baptized man who receives the Sacrament of Holy Orders. Priests work with their bishops. The priest teaches about the Catholic faith. He celebrates Mass. Priests help to guide the Church.

Who is a deacon?

A deacon is ordained to help bishops and priests. He is not a priest. He is ordained to serve the Church.

What is the Sacrament of Matrimony?

In the Sacrament of Matrimony, or Marriage, a baptized man and a baptized woman make a lifelong promise. They promise to serve the Church as a married couple. They promise to love each other. They show Christ's love to others.

What are the sacramentals of the Church?

Sacramentals are objects and blessings the Church uses. They help us worship God.

Life in the Spirit

The Moral Life

Why did God create us?

God created us to give honor and glory to him. God created us to live a life of blessing with him here on Earth and forever in Heaven.

What does it mean to live a moral life?

God wants us to be happy. He gives us the gift of his grace. When we accept God's gift by living the way Jesus taught us, we are being moral.

What is the Great Commandment?

Jesus taught us to love God above all else. He taught us to love our neighbors as ourselves. This is the path to happiness.

What are the Ten Commandments?

The Ten Commandments are the laws that God gave Moses. They teach us to live as God's people. They teach us to love God, others, and ourselves. The Commandments are written on the hearts of all people.

What are the Beatitudes?

The Beatitudes are teachings of Jesus. They tell us what real happiness is. The Beatitudes tell us about the Kingdom of God. They help us live as followers of Jesus. They help us keep God at the center of our lives.

What are the Works of Mercy?

God's love and kindness is at work in the world. This is what mercy is. Human works of mercy are acts of loving kindness. We reach out to people. We help them with what they need for their bodies and their spirits.

What are the precepts of the Church?

The precepts of the Church are five rules. These rules help us worship God and grow in love of God and our neighbors.

Holiness of Life and Grace

What is holiness?

Holiness is life with God. Holy people are in right relationship with God, with people, and with all of creation.

What is grace?

Grace is the gift of God sharing his life and love with us.

What is sanctifying grace?

Sanctifying grace is the grace we receive at Baptism. It is a free gift of God, given by the Holy Spirit.

What are the Gifts of the Holy Spirit?

The seven Gifts of the Holy Spirit help us to live our Baptism. They are wisdom, understanding, right judgment, courage, knowledge, reverence, and wonder and awe.

The Virtues

What are the virtues?

The virtues are spiritual powers or habits. The virtues help us to do what is good.

What are the most important virtues?

The most important virtues are the three virtues of faith, hope, and love. These virtues are gifts from God. They help us keep God at the center of our lives.

What is conscience?

Every person has a conscience. It is a gift God gives to every person. It helps us know and judge what is right and what is wrong. Our consciences move us to do good and avoid evil.

Evil and Sin

What is evil?

Evil is the harm we choose to do to one another and to God's creation.

What is temptation?

Temptations are feelings, people, and things that try to get us to turn away from God's love and not live a holy life.

What is sin?

Sin is freely choosing to do or say something that we know God does not want us to do or say.

What is mortal sin?

A mortal sin is doing or saying something on purpose that is very bad. A mortal sin is against what God wants us to do or say. When we commit a mortal sin, we lose sanctifying grace.

What are venial sins?

Venial sins are sins that are less serious than mortal sins. They weaken our love for God and for one another. They make us less holy.

Christian Prayer

What is prayer?

Prayer is talking to and listening to God. When we pray, we raise our minds and hearts to God the Father, Son, and Holy Spirit.

What is the Our Father?

The Lord's Prayer, or Our Father, is the prayer of all Christians. Jesus taught his disciples the Our Father. Jesus gave this prayer to the Church. When we pray the Our Father, we come closer to God and to his Son, Jesus Christ. The Our Father helps us become like Jesus.

What kinds of prayer are there?

Some kinds of prayer use words that we say aloud or quietly in our hearts. Some silent prayers use our imagination to bring us closer to God. Another silent prayer is simply being with God.

Glossary

A

almighty [page 37]

God alone is almighty. This means that only God has the power to do everything good.

Ascension [page 65]

The Ascension is the return of the Risen Jesus to his Father in Heaven forty days after the Resurrection.

assembly [page 121]

The assembly is the People of God gathered to celebrate Mass. All members of the assembly share in the celebration of Mass.

B

Baptism [page 93]

Baptism is the Sacrament that joins us to Christ and makes us members of the Church. We receive the gift of the Holy Spirit and become adopted sons and daughters of God.

believe [page 21]

To believe in God means to know God and to give ourselves to him with all our hearts.

Bible [page 13]

The Bible is the written Word of God.

Body of Christ [page 73]

The Church is the Body of Christ. Jesus Christ is the Head of the Church. All the baptized are members of the Church.

C

Communion of Saints [page 73]

The Church is the Communion of Saints. The Church is the unity of all the faithful followers of Jesus on Earth and those in Heaven.

compassion [page 128]

Compassion means to care about others when they are hurt or feeling sad. Having compassion makes us want to help them feel better.

Confirmation [page 101]

Confirmation is the Sacrament in which the gift of the Holy Spirit strengthens us to live our Baptism.

conscience [page 201]

Conscience is a gift from God that helps us to make wise choices.

consequences [page 201]

Consequences are the good or bad things that happen after we make choices.

courage [page 144]

We receive the gift of courage from the Holy Spirit at Baptism. This gift helps us choose to do what is good.

Covenant [page 49]

The Covenant is God's promise to always love and be kind to his people.

covet [page 181]

We covet when we have an unhealthy desire for something.

Creator [page 37]

God alone is the Creator. God made everyone and everything out of love and without any help.

Crucifixion [page 57]

The Crucifixion is the Death of Jesus on a cross.

D

disciples [page 13]

Disciples are people who follow and learn from someone. Disciples of Jesus follow and learn from him.

E

Eucharist [page 137]

The Eucharist is the Sacrament of the Body and Blood of Jesus Christ.

F

faith [page 21]

Faith is a gift from God that makes us able to believe in him.

[page 92]

The virtue of faith is a gift from God. It gives us the power to come to know God and believe in him.

false witness [page 181]

Giving false witness means telling lies.

forgiveness [page 108]

Forgiveness is a sign of love. We ask for forgiveness because we love God. We want everything to be right again. We share God's forgiving love with others when we forgive people who hurt us.

fortitude [page 164]

Fortitude is another word for courage. Fortitude helps us stay strong, to do our best, and to do what is right and good when it's hard to do so. The Holy Spirit gives us the gift of fortitude to live the way that God wants us to live.

G

generosity [page 64]

You show generosity when you use the gifts you received from God to help others.

goodness [page 72]

Goodness is a sign that we are living our Baptism. When we are good to people, we show that we know they are children of God. When we are good to people, we honor God.

grace [page 93]

Grace is the gift of God sharing his life with us and helping us live as his children.

Great Commandment [page 165]

The Great Commandment is to love God above all else and to love others as we love ourselves.

H

Heaven [page 193]

Heaven is happiness forever with God and all the Saints.

Holy Trinity [page 29]

The Holy Trinity is One God in Three Divine Person—God the Father, God the Son, and God the Holy Spirit.

honor [page 36]

When we honor others, we show respect and value them. We honor God because we are proud to be his children.

[page 157]

To honor someone is to treat them with kindness, respect, and love.

hope [page 216]

Hope is trusting that God hears us, cares about us, and will care for us.

hospitality [page 20]

Jesus tells us to treat all people with hospitality. Hospitality helps us welcome others as God's children. It helps us treat others with dignity and respect.

humility [page 192]

Humility helps us to recognize that all we are and all we have comes from God. We are humble when we choose to follow God's ways and make them our own.

J

Jesus Christ [page 49]

Jesus Christ is the Son of God. He is the Second Person of the Holy Trinity who became one of us. Jesus is true God and true man.

joy [page 200]

Joy is one of the Fruits of the Holy Spirit. Joy shows that we are thankful for God's love and for all God has made. Joy shows that we enjoy life and delight in making others joyful.

justice [page 180]

We practice justice when we do our very best to always be fair to others.

K

kindness [page 156]

We act with kindness when we do things that show we care. We are kind when we treat other people as we want to be treated.

Kingdom of God [page 217]

The Kingdom of God is also called the Kingdom of Heaven.

knowledge [page 100]

Knowledge is one of the Gifts of the Holy Spirit. Knowledge helps us better hear and understand the meaning of the Word of God.

L

Liturgy of the Eucharist [page 137]

The Liturgy of the Eucharist is the second main part of the Mass. The Church does what Jesus did at the Last Supper.

Liturgy of the Word [page 129]

The Liturgy of the Word is the first main part of the Mass. God speaks to us through readings from the Bible.

love [page 120]

Love is the greatest of all virtues. Love gives us the power to cherish God above all things. It also gives us the power to serve people for the sake of God.

Mass [page 121]

The Mass is the most important celebration of the Church. At Mass, we gather to worship God. We listen to God's Word. We celebrate and share in the Eucharist.

mercy [page 48]

Jesus said, "Blessed are people of mercy." Mercy helps us act with kindness toward others, no matter what.

obedience [page 172]

Authority is a gift from God. God gives people authority to help us follow God's laws. People in authority, such as parents and grandparents, teachers and principals, priests and bishops, deserve respect. The virtue of obedience gives us strength to honor and respect people in authority.

penance [page 109]

Penance is something we do or say to show we are truly sorry for the choices we made to hurt someone.

Pentecost [page 65]

Pentecost is the day the Holy Spirit came to the disciples of Jesus fifty days after the Resurrection.

piety [page 84]

Piety is a Gift of the Holy Spirit. Piety is the love we have for God. That love makes us want to worship and give God thanks and praise.

procession [page 145]

A procession is people prayerfully walking together. It is a prayer in action.

R

rabbi [page 165]

Rabbi is a Hebrew word that means teacher.

reconciliation [page 109]

Reconciliation means to become friends again.

respect [page 12]

When we pay attention to what others say to us, we show them respect. Listening is a sign of respect and can help us learn well. Respect for others is a way we show God's love.

Resurrection [page 57]

The Resurrection is God the Father raising Jesus from the dead to new life.

S

Sacraments [page 85]

The Sacraments are the seven signs of God's love for us that Jesus gave the Church. We share in God's love when we celebrate the Sacraments.

sacrifice [page 56]

You sacrifice when you give up something because you love someone. Jesus sacrificed his life for all people. Followers of Jesus make sacrifices out of love for God and for people.

sanctifying grace [page 209]

Sanctifying grace is the gift of God sharing his life with us.

sin [page 109]

Sin is freely choosing to do or say something we know God does not want us to do or say.

soul [page 29]

Our soul is that part of us that lives forever.

spiritual gifts [page 101]

The Holy Spirit gives us spiritual gifts to help us love and serve other people. We use the spiritual gifts to show our love for God.

T

Ten Commandments [page 173]

The Ten Commandments are the laws that God gave Moses. They teach us to live as God's people. They help us live happy and holy lives.

thankfulness [page 136]

Thankfulness is a big part of who we are as disciples of Jesus. We have received wonderful blessings and gifts. Jesus calls us to be a thankful people.

trust [page 208]

When we trust people, we know we can rely on them. We can depend on them to help us when we are in need.

W

wise choices [page 193]

Wise choices help us to live as followers of God.

wonder [page 28]

Wonder is a Gift of the Holy Spirit. It helps us see God's greatness and discover more about God. It then moves us to praise him.

worship [page 85]

Worship means to honor and love God above all else.

Index

Credits